The Art of Wellness

How to Find, Live, & Stay Mentally Fit

By Kevin Hines

The Art of Wellness

How to Find, Live, & Stay Mentally Fit

Table of Contents

Chapter 1: 7

The Road to Mental Fitness 7

Chapter 2: 18

Understanding Mental Fitness 18

Chapter 3: 28

Breaking Free from Labels 28

Chapter 4: 34

Building Mental Resilience – How to Turn Struggles into Strength 34

Chapter 5: 40

The Power of Routine – Structure as a Lifeline 40

Chapter 6: 47

Nutrition and the Brain – Fueling Mental Health 47

Chapter 7: 55

Exercise for the Mind and Body – Moving Toward Wellness 55

Chapter 8: 61

Sleep as Medicine – Restoring the Mind 61

Chapter 9: 67

Mindfulness and Meditation – Learning to Be Present 67

Chapter 10: 74

Emotional Intelligence – Understanding and Controlling Your Emotions 74

Chapter 11: 81

The Role of Social Connection – Why We Need Each Other 81

Chapter 12: 88

The Art of Letting Go – Releasing What No Longer Serves You 88

Chapter 13: 95

The Power of Purpose – Turning Pain into Passion 95

Chapter 14 102

The Power of Self-Compassion – Learning to Love Yourself Again 102

Chapter 15: 109

Mastering Brain Health, Physical Health, and Overall Well-Being – The Work of a Lifetime 109

Chapter 16: 116

Resilience – The Art of Bouncing Back Stronger 116

Chapter 17: 123

Unbreakable – The Strength Within You 123

Chapter 18: 131

The Greatest Gift – Living to Give Back 131

This book will serve as a powerful, engaging, and life-changing guide.

Introduction to The Art of Wellness

Hello and welcome, my friend. My name is Kevin Hines, and I'm both humbled and honored that you've picked up this book. My journey to mental fitness has been anything but simple—it's been filled with harsh lessons, profound realizations, moments of hopelessness, and, ultimately, the revelation that a life worth living is one built on resilience, purpose, and unwavering hope.

In 2000, I survived a suicidal act that should have ended my life. I stood on the edge of the Golden Gate Bridge convinced there was no way forward. My mind was clouded by insurmountable darkness and overwhelming "brain pain." But in the very moment my hands left that rail, I realized my life was not meant to end—at least not that day. That second chance became the catalyst for the work I do now: sharing tools, resources, and stories that remind all of us that hope is real, help exists, and that every single one of us deserves a future.

The chapters ahead are the culmination of what I've learned in my ongoing life with bipolar disorder, suicidal ideation, and the daily effort to maintain my brain and mental fitness. But more than that, this book is a testament to the idea that none of us are defined by our darkest days. We are not the labels thrust upon us, nor are we the diagnoses that sometimes feel as if they consume us. Instead, we are extraordinary beings capable of transformation, resilience, and incredible feats of courage.

What You'll Find Here:

- **Real-Life Insights:** The lessons in these here come from hard-earned experience—mine and countless others who've walked alongside me in the mental health community.
- **Practical Tools:** Each chapter provides actionable steps, routines, and techniques you can integrate into your daily life to bolster your mental, emotional, physical, and spiritual well-being.
- **A Focus on Holistic Wellness:** True mental fitness isn't about "fixing" only one aspect of ourselves. It's about nurturing the body, mind, relationships, and sense of purpose that together form a meaningful life.
- **Hope and Connection:** I have lived both in the darkest of nights and in the radiant possibility of the next dawn. My greatest wish is that you discover that no matter how heavy your burdens feel, light is always within reach.

As you embark on this journey, remember: Your story matters. You are here for a reason. Whether you're searching for answers, strength, or a spark of hope, I believe this book can help guide you toward the life you deserve—one filled with possibility, growth, and the unwavering knowledge that you are worthy of every breath you take. Thank you for letting me be a part of your pursuit of wellness. Each step you take forward—no matter how small—moves you closer to a more resilient mind, a healthier body, and a purpose-driven life. And that, my friend, is worth every ounce of effort you can give.

With gratitude and a steadfast belief in your future,

Kevin Hines (replace with my signature)

Chapter 1:

The Road to Mental Fitness

Setting Out on the Journey

Mental fitness is not a destination—it's a lifelong expedition. Like training for a marathon, nurturing your mind requires daily commitment, practice, and the willingness to embrace both victory and setback. In my early years, I struggled in silence, weighed down by feelings of despair and confusion. I often wondered if I would ever find a way to break free from the darkness. That question sparked a journey of self-discovery that transformed my life. In this chapter, I invite you to join me on that road. I share how I learned to build mental strength step by step, combining practical techniques with personal insights. The first step on this path is acknowledging that every moment offers a new opportunity for growth. With that in mind, let's begin our journey by examining the foundation of mental fitness.

Recognizing the Need for Change

I still remember the day I realized I needed help. I was living in the middle of a storm—emotionally and mentally—and felt as if I were drowning. Then due to this storm, I almost literally drowned. In that moment, I decided to take a stand. I recognized that brain and mental fitness is as important as physical fitness, and just like you wouldn't ignore liver, heart, lung, or kidney disease, you cannot ignore a hurting mind.

Steps to Recognize the Need for Change:

1. **Self-Reflection:** Begin by asking yourself, "How do I really feel?" Journaling my emotions daily became a powerful tool for reflection. I discovered patterns that alerted me when I was nearing a breaking point.
2. **Mindful Observation:** Notice the subtle signals your body sends—a tightening in your chest, a restless mind, or fatigue that lingers despite sleep. These physical cues often mirror internal struggles.
3. **Acceptance:** Embrace the fact that feeling unwell is not a personal failing. I learned that acknowledging my pain was the first courageous act toward healing.

Taking that step required bravery, but it also opened the door to learning techniques that would eventually help me regain control. Accepting the need for change was the catalyst for my transformation.

My Story—From Darkness to Light

There was a time when my world felt void of color—a monotonous existence punctuated by anxiety and depression. I was caught in a loop of negative thoughts, paranoia, and overwhelming self-doubt. At my lowest, I reached out for help and discovered that my pain was shared by many, and that recovery was possible.

The Turning Point:

- **A Moment of Clarity:** One cold morning, as I sat alone, I realized that every day I survived was evidence of my inner strength. I decided to rewrite my narrative from victimhood to resilience.
- **Seeking Support:** I began talking with mental health professionals who helped me understand that my mind, like any muscle, could be trained.

Therapy introduced me to techniques like Cognitive Behavioral Therapy (CBT), which reframed my destructive thoughts.
- **Small Victories:** Each day brought tiny wins—a moment of peace during meditation, a burst of energy after a walk, or the simple act of writing down a positive thought. These victories built a foundation for my recovery.

This personal transformation taught me that mental fitness is a series of incremental steps—a patchwork of breakthroughs that, over time, add up to profound change.

Laying the Groundwork for Mental Fitness

Building mental fitness starts with creating a solid foundation. Just as a house needs a strong base, your mind requires a structured approach that blends self-awareness, self-care, and practical strategies.

Key Elements of a Strong Foundation:

- **Routine and Structure:** Establishing a consistent daily routine creates a sense of stability. I began with simple practices: a morning meditation, a healthy breakfast, and a daily walk. Over time, these rituals became the scaffolding of my mental strength.
- **Physical Health:** The mind and body are inextricably linked. Regular exercise, nutritious food, and adequate sleep form the pillars that support mental well-being.
- **Mindfulness Practice:** Learning to focus on the present moment reduced my anxiety and increased my clarity. Techniques such as mindful breathing helped me anchor my thoughts and maintain balance.

- **Community and Connection:** I found solace in sharing my journey with others. Whether through therapy groups, supportive friends, or online communities, connection provided both accountability and empathy.

By integrating these elements into my life, I slowly began to see the contours of a healthier, more resilient mind.

The Daily Discipline of Self-Care

One of the most crucial lessons I learned was that mental fitness demands daily discipline. Self-care isn't a luxury—it's a necessity. I discovered that small, consistent actions could profoundly affect my mental health.

Daily Self-Care Rituals:

- **Morning Rituals:** I started each day with a quiet moment of reflection. Whether it was through meditation, reading a motivational quote, or simply enjoying a cup of tea, this ritual set a positive tone for the day.
- **Journaling:** Writing down my thoughts allowed me to externalize my internal struggles. I tracked my mood, noted triggers, and celebrated my progress—even on days when progress felt invisible.
- **Mindful Movement:** Incorporating even brief periods of physical activity—like stretching or a brisk walk—helped me stay connected to my body and clear my mind.
- **Rest and Rejuvenation:** I learned that rest is not a sign of weakness. Setting aside time to relax, indulge in a hobby, or simply do nothing was essential for recharging my mental energy.

By committing to these daily practices, I began to see improvements in my emotional resilience and overall sense of well-being.

Embracing Vulnerability and Authenticity

One of the most empowering steps on my journey was learning to embrace vulnerability. For a long time, I believed that showing my true self was a weakness. It was the key to unlocking deeper connections and genuine healing.

How Vulnerability Transforms Mental Fitness:

- **Authentic Expression:** I started sharing my story with trusted friends and mentors. This act of opening up reduced my isolation and allowed me to receive support and encouragement.
- **Self-Acceptance:** Accepting my vulnerabilities meant acknowledging that I was not perfect—and that was okay. By recognizing my imperfections, I began to treat myself with more compassion.
- **Building Resilience:** Vulnerability taught me that it's not about never falling but about learning to rise each time I do. Every time I allowed myself to be open, I grew stronger.
- **Connection and Empathy:** When I shared my struggles, I discovered that many people were fighting similar battles. This realization fostered a sense of community and mutual understanding, reinforcing the idea that I was never truly alone.

Embracing vulnerability was transformative. It shifted my mindset from fear to empowerment and taught me that true strength lies in our ability to be honest with ourselves and others.

Strategies for Overcoming Setbacks

The journey to mental fitness is not linear. Setbacks are inevitable, but they do not define your path. I encountered many stumbling blocks along the way—from days when even getting out of bed felt impossible, to moments when my old patterns of negativity resurfaced.

Strategies I Used to Overcome Setbacks:

- **Reframing Failure:** I learned to view setbacks not as failures, but as opportunities to learn. Each challenge was a lesson in resilience, a chance to understand my triggers better and adjust my approach.
- **Crisis Management Techniques:** In moments of acute distress, I relied on techniques such as deep breathing, grounding exercises, and reaching out to a trusted friend. These tools helped me regain control when emotions threatened to overwhelm me.
- **Flexibility in Routine:** Understanding that perfection is unattainable allowed me to adapt my self-care routines. On difficult days, I modified my activities to match my energy levels without abandoning the commitment to my well-being.
- **Seeking Professional Guidance:** There were times when I needed additional support from mental health professionals. Therapy provided a safe space to process my setbacks and devise new strategies for moving forward.
- **Celebrating Small Wins:** Even on the toughest days, I focused on small victories—like completing a short walk or writing a few lines in my journal. These minor successes accumulated into a broader sense of progress.

By adopting these strategies, I transformed setbacks into steppingstones, each one a part of my larger journey toward lasting mental fitness.

Cultivating a Resilient Mindset

A resilient mindset is the cornerstone of mental fitness. I realized early on that how I perceived my struggles would determine the course of my recovery. A fixed mindset led me to feel trapped by my challenges, while a growth mindset empowered me to see every obstacle as a chance to evolve.

Key Elements in Building a Resilient Mindset:

- **Growth Over Fixed:** Embrace challenges as opportunities to learn. Each hardship has taught me valuable lessons about my strengths and areas for improvement.
- **Positive Self-Talk:** Replacing self-criticism with affirmations helped me shift my inner dialogue. I would remind myself daily, "I am capable. I am worthy. I will overcome it."
- **Visualization:** I often pictured myself emerging stronger from each trial. Visualizing a brighter future provided the motivation I needed to persevere during difficult times.
- **Learning from Role Models:** Reading about others who overcame adversity—friends, mentors, and even historical figures—reinforced my belief that recovery was possible. Their stories became fuel for my own journey.
- **Mindfulness and Reflection:** Regular mindfulness practices kept me grounded in the present, reducing the tendency to catastrophize future challenges.

These elements combined to form a resilient mindset that empowered me to navigate life's unpredictable twists with courage and hope.

Integrating Lessons into Daily Life

Transforming insights into actionable habits was essential. It wasn't enough to understand mental fitness in theory; I needed to integrate these lessons into my everyday life.

Daily Integration Techniques:

- **Structured Reflection:** Each evening, I dedicated time to reflect on the day's experiences. I noted what went well, what could be improved, and how I felt in each moment. This practice helped me adjust my approach and set intentions for the following day.
- **Goal Setting:** I set realistic, daily goals that aligned with my broader vision of mental wellness. Whether it was committing to five minutes of meditation or reaching out to a friend, every goal was a building block for my overall progress.
- **Habit Stacking:** I paired new habits with established ones. For instance, I would journal right after my morning cup of tea—a routine that eventually became second nature.
- **Feedback Loop:** I created a feedback loop by discussing my progress with my therapist and supportive friends. Their insights provided fresh perspectives and helped me refine my strategies.
- **Celebration and Gratitude:** Celebrating progress, no matter how small, nurtured a sense of accomplishment. I kept a gratitude list, recording moments of joy and strength throughout the day.

By embedding these practices into my daily routine, I gradually built a life where mental fitness was not a fleeting effort but an enduring way of being.

The Role of Self-Discovery

Understanding who I truly was played a vital role in my journey. Self-discovery is a continuous process, one that deepens over time as you uncover layers of your identity, dreams, and aspirations.

My Journey of Self-Discovery Included:

- **Exploring My Passions:** I reconnected with hobbies I had long neglected—music, art, and writing. Each creative outlet became a mirror reflecting parts of myself that I had forgotten.
- **Challenging My Beliefs:** I questioned long-held beliefs that contributed to my negative self-image. Through therapy and reflective reading, I began to dismantle those limiting narratives.
- **Building a Personal Philosophy:** I crafted a personal philosophy that centered on growth, compassion, and resilience. This philosophy guided my decisions and provided a steady anchor during turbulent times.
- **Mindful Exploration:** I made it a point to explore new ideas and experiences—whether through books, travel, or conversations with diverse individuals. These explorations enriched my understanding of the world and my place within it.

Self-discovery not only empowered me but also made the journey toward mental fitness deeply personal and uniquely rewarding.

Celebrating the Journey

It is important to celebrate every milestone along the path. I learned that acknowledgment of progress is a powerful motivator. Celebrating success—no matter how incremental—nurtures hope and inspires continued effort.

Ways to Celebrate:

- **Personal Rituals:** I created small celebrations for myself—a favorite song, a special treat, or even a quiet moment of reflection—to honor my achievements.
- **Sharing Victories:** I learned to share my successes with loved ones. Their encouragement reminded me that every step forward was a collective triumph.
- **Reflective Reviews:** Regularly reviewing my journey helped me appreciate how far I'd come. Looking back on my journal entries and the obstacles I had overcome reinforced my commitment to continued growth.
- **Mindful Appreciation:** Taking time to simply be present and grateful for the progress made nurtured my mental well-being. Celebrating the journey, not just the destination, became a cornerstone of my philosophy.

Every step, every setback turned into a lesson, and every lesson transformed into a strength. Celebrating the journey instilled in me the belief that no matter how slow the progress, I was moving forward—and that was cause for celebration.

A New Beginning Every Day

The road to mental fitness is ongoing, and each day presents a fresh start. I learned that every sunrise is an opportunity to begin again, to refine your habits, and to approach life with renewed energy and determination.

Reflections for Chapter 1:

- **Commitment to Growth:** Mental fitness is a commitment that requires constant nurturing. Embrace each day as a new chance to practice self-care, resilience, and mindfulness.
- **Empowerment Through Action:** My journey taught me that empowerment comes from taking action—no matter how small. With every mindful decision and every self-care ritual, I reclaimed a piece of my strength.
- **Invitation to the Reader:** I invite you now to take these lessons to heart. Reflect on your own journey, identify small areas for improvement, and remember that every step, every effort, builds toward a resilient, vibrant mind.

As we close this chapter, remember: the road to mental fitness is filled with both challenges and triumphs. Your journey is uniquely yours, and every day is a chance to build a healthier, more empowered version of yourself. This chapter not only recounts my personal journey from darkness to light but also provides concrete steps, reflective practices, and inspirational insights for you to begin your own path to mental fitness. The coming chapters will build on these foundations, each offering additional tools, narratives, and practical strategies to help you live a more resilient and fulfilling life.

Chapter 2:

Understanding Mental Fitness

What Is Mental Fitness?

Mental fitness is much more than simply having a "good day" or feeling happy for a moment—it is the deliberate practice of nurturing and strengthening the mind in much the same way you would build physical strength. In my own journey, I discovered that my mental well-being depended on understanding and embracing the complexity of my thoughts, emotions, and behaviors. Mental fitness involves emotional regulation, cognitive flexibility, self-awareness, and self-care. It is about training your mind to be resilient in the face of adversity, adaptable when circumstances change, and proactive about maintaining balance. This understanding laid the groundwork for me to move beyond the notion that mental health is only for those in crisis, and embrace it as a lifelong, dynamic practice.

The Brain as a Muscle

Imagine your brain as a muscle that can be trained. Neuroplasticity—the brain's ability to rewire itself—taught me that every thought and action contributes to my mental strength. Early in my recovery, I learned that the repeated practice of positive habits could reshape my neural pathways and help me overcome negative patterns.

- **Building New Pathways:** Just as you strengthen your body through exercise, you can "exercise" your mind. Each time I practiced mindfulness, reframed a negative thought, or engaged in self-reflection; I was actively creating new, healthier neural circuits.
- **Consistency Is Key:** Just as muscles grow with regular training, mental resilience deepens through daily, consistent effort. Even small, repeated actions—like taking five minutes to breathe deeply—compound over time to build lasting mental strength.

This concept of neuroplasticity empowered me to believe that I was not fixed in my struggles, but that I could evolve and grow, no matter how entrenched my old patterns seemed.

The Components of Mental Fitness

Understanding mental fitness means breaking it down into its core components. Through my own experiences, I learned that mental health is multi-faceted and requires attention on several levels:

- **Emotional Regulation:** The ability to manage and respond to emotions in a healthy way is crucial. I discovered that labeling and accepting my emotions, rather than suppressing them, allowed me to handle stress more effectively.
- **Cognitive Flexibility:** The capacity to shift perspective and adapt to change helped me move away from rigid thinking. I started challenging my assumptions and embracing alternative viewpoints, which was liberating.
- **Self-Awareness:** Knowing yourself—your triggers, strengths, and areas for growth—is a cornerstone of mental fitness. Through journaling and reflective practices, I became more in tune with my inner world.

- **Self-Care Practices:** Just as physical health requires balanced nutrition and exercise, mental health needs daily habits such as mindfulness, adequate sleep, and nurturing social connections.

Each component plays a vital role in building a resilient mind and understanding them helped me tailor my own wellness practices to my unique needs.

The Journey Toward Self-Awareness

For many years, I operated on autopilot, unaware of the subtle ways my thoughts and habits were sabotaging my well-being. The turning point came when I began to practice deep self-awareness. I started by asking myself difficult questions and honestly confronting my internal dialogue.

- **Journaling for Clarity:** I dedicated time each day to record my thoughts, feelings, and behaviors. This practice revealed patterns I had long ignored—both positive and negative.
- **Mindful Observation:** I learned to watch my thoughts as they arose, without judgment. This non-reactive awareness allowed me to spot unhelpful thought patterns and gently steer them toward more constructive paths.
- **Reflective Practices:** Whether through meditation or quiet walks in nature, I engaged in activities that helped me explore my inner landscape. Over time, this self-discovery became a powerful tool for growth.

Embracing self-awareness enabled me to understand my triggers and build strategies to manage them, laying the foundation for a more resilient and empowered self.

Emotional Resilience in Action

Emotional resilience is the capacity to bounce back after life's inevitable setbacks. In my darkest moments, I realized that resilience wasn't about never falling—it was about finding the strength to rise each time I did.

- **Learning to Feel:** I began by acknowledging my emotions, even the painful ones. Allowing myself to feel without immediately trying to escape the discomfort was a radical act of self-compassion.
- **Developing Coping Strategies:** Over time, I honed various techniques—from deep breathing and visualization to reaching out for support—that helped me weather emotional storms.
- **Transforming Pain:** Each setback became a lesson. I discovered that the challenges I faced were not signs of weakness but opportunities to learn and grow.
- **Building a Support System:** Surrounding myself with trusted individuals provided a network of encouragement, helping me see that resilience is often nurtured through community.

These experiences taught me that emotional resilience is a skill that grows stronger with every challenge you overcome.

Cognitive Flexibility—Embracing Change

Cognitive flexibility—the ability to adjust your thinking in response to new information or changing circumstances—has been a key factor in my mental fitness journey. There were times when rigid, negative thought patterns held me captive. Learning to adapt and shift my mindset was liberating.

- **Questioning Assumptions:** I made it a habit to question my automatic thoughts. Whenever I caught myself in a negative loop, I asked, "Is there another way to see this?"
- **Embracing Uncertainty:** Life is unpredictable, and learning to accept that uncertainty is part of the human experience helped reduce my anxiety. I started viewing uncertainty as an invitation to explore new possibilities.
- **Flexible Problem-Solving:** Adapting my strategies as circumstances changed allowed me to overcome obstacles more efficiently. For instance, when a particular routine stopped working, I wasn't afraid to try a new approach.
- **Mindset Shifts:** I practiced reframing challenges as opportunities for growth. This shift in perspective transformed many difficult situations into steppingstones toward greater resilience.

By developing cognitive flexibility, I not only broadened my perspective but also unlocked new avenues for personal and mental growth.

The Role of Self-Care in Mental Fitness

Self-care is the lifeblood of mental fitness. In my journey, I learned that neglecting self-care only exacerbated my struggles. I began to see self-care as a non-negotiable part of my daily routine—a necessary investment in my future.

- **Prioritizing Rest:** I discovered that quality sleep was essential for cognitive function and emotional balance. Establishing a regular sleep schedule became one of my top priorities.
- **Mindfulness and Meditation:** Incorporating mindfulness into my day helped me stay centered. Whether through a guided meditation or simply taking a moment to focus on my breath, these practices grounded me in the present.

- **Physical Activity:** I made time for exercise, understanding that a healthy body supports a healthy mind. Even short walks or stretching sessions had a profound impact on my mood.
- **Nutrition and Hydration:** Eating a balanced diet and staying hydrated was another cornerstone of my self-care routine. I noticed that when I nourished my body, my mind responded positively.

Self-care isn't selfish—it's the foundation upon which mental fitness is built. By consistently investing in my well-being, I started to see significant improvements in my mood, energy, and overall outlook.

Bridging Science and Experience

While my personal journey provided the emotional motivation for change, scientific insights offered the practical tools I needed. Understanding the research behind mental fitness empowered me to take control of my recovery.

- **The Science of Neuroplasticity:** Studies show that our brains are capable of change at any age. This gave me hope, knowing that the patterns I had developed were not permanent and could be reshaped with practice.
- **Evidence-Based Practices:** Techniques such as Cognitive Behavioral Therapy (CBT) and mindfulness meditation are backed by research demonstrating their effectiveness in reducing anxiety, depression, and stress.
- **The Role of Nutrition:** Emerging research in nutritional psychiatry reinforced my belief in the connection between diet and mental health. Foods rich in omega-3 fatty acids, for example, have been linked to improved mood and cognitive function.

- **Holistic Approaches:** Combining traditional therapeutic techniques with complementary practices like yoga and meditation provided a comprehensive approach to my mental fitness.

By bridging the gap between science and personal experience, I was able to build a toolkit that was both deeply personal and grounded in proven methods.

Educational Pathways to Mental Fitness

Learning about mental fitness is an ongoing journey. I immersed myself in books, seminars, and workshops that broadened my understanding of how to care for my mind.

- **Self-Help Literature:** I devoured books on psychology, mindfulness, and self-care. Each new piece of knowledge added another tool to my mental fitness arsenal.
- **Workshops and Seminars:** Attending seminars allowed me to learn from experts and connect with others on similar journeys. These experiences fostered a sense of community and shared purpose.
- **Online Communities:** The digital world provided access to forums and groups where I could exchange ideas, share experiences, and find support. The collective wisdom of these communities was invaluable.
- **Formal Education:** In some cases, I even enrolled in courses that delved deeper into neuroscience and psychology. Understanding the mechanics of the mind gave me a greater appreciation for the changes I was making.

Education isn't just about absorbing facts—it's about empowering yourself to take control of your mental health. Every lesson I learned built my confidence and deepened my commitment to mental fitness.

Integrating Personal Stories with Learning

What makes the journey to mental fitness so transformative is the integration of personal experience with new knowledge. I began to see every setback and breakthrough as part of a larger narrative—one that was uniquely mine yet universally relatable.

- **Personal Anecdotes:** I shared stories of both my struggles and triumphs. Whether it was the breakthrough moment during a meditation session or the profound impact of a supportive conversation, each experience taught me something new.
- **Learning Through Reflection:** I often revisited my journal entries to reflect on how far I'd come. These reflections helped me connect the dots between theory and practice, reinforcing the importance of every lesson learned.
- **Sharing with Others:** Telling my story not only empowered me but also resonated with others. The exchange of personal narratives created a ripple effect, inspiring mutual growth and understanding.
- **Translating Knowledge into Action:** The educational insights I gained were never left as abstract ideas. I applied them directly to my daily routines, transforming theoretical knowledge into practical strategies for well-being.

This synthesis of personal story and academic insight became a powerful catalyst for change, driving home the point that mental fitness is both a personal journey and a shared human experience.

Empowerment Through Understanding

As I deepened my understanding of mental fitness, I found that knowledge itself was incredibly empowering. Realizing that I had the capacity to change my thought patterns, regulate my emotions, and nurture my mind instilled in me a renewed sense of purpose.

- **Empowering Beliefs:** I replaced limiting beliefs with empowering ones. I began to see challenges not as insurmountable obstacles, but as opportunities to exercise and strengthen my mental resolve.
- **A Sense of Control:** Understanding the mechanics of my mind gave me a sense of control over my life. I wasn't merely at the mercy of my thoughts and emotions—I was actively shaping my mental landscape.
- **Inspiration to Others:** As I grew more confident, I discovered that sharing my insights could help others feel less alone. Empowerment is contagious; when you understand that change is possible, it inspires those around you to embark on their own journeys.
- **Lifelong Commitment:** Recognizing mental fitness as an ongoing process transformed my approach to life. Every day became an opportunity to learn, grow, and fortify my mental well-being.

With every new understanding, I felt more equipped to face life's challenges and more determined to help others realize their own potential.

Moving Forward with Purpose

The journey of understanding mental fitness is both a personal evolution and a call to action. It has reshaped the way I view my struggles and successes, and it continues to inform every decision I make.

- **Daily Intentions:** Each morning, I set an intention to nurture my mental well-being. This simple act of mindfulness has helped me stay grounded and focused on my long-term goals.
- **A Call to Action:** I invite you to begin your own journey of understanding mental fitness. Embrace self-awareness, question your assumptions, and commit to practices that strengthen your mind.
- **Integration into Daily Life:** The insights shared in this chapter are not meant to be read once and forgotten. They are tools to be revisited, refined, and integrated into your everyday routine.
- **A Future of Growth:** As you move forward, remember that every step you take—no matter how small—is an investment in a healthier, more resilient future. Your journey is ongoing, and each day offers new lessons, new challenges, and new opportunities for growth.

In understanding mental fitness, I found not just a method for survival, but a way to thrive. This chapter has laid the intellectual and emotional groundwork for what comes next, empowering you with the knowledge to transform your mental landscape and set the stage for lasting well-being.

Chapter 3:

Breaking Free from Labels

The Power of Labels and the Damage of Self-Descrimination

Words are powerful. The labels we attach to ourselves, or that others attach to us, can shape our identity, limit our potential, and dictate how we see ourselves in the world. This is especially true when it comes to brain and mental health. For years, I lived under the weight of labels—some given to me by medical professionals, some by society, and some I unknowingly placed on myself. Words like "bipolar," "broken," "suicidal," and "unstable" became chains that held me back. They weren't just words; they were definitions I felt trapped within. The stigma of mental illness was not just external—it was something I had internalized.

Self-descrimination is one of the most insidious barriers to mental wellness. It is the voice in your head that says:

- You are your diagnosis.
- You will never be more than your struggles.
- You are weak, unworthy, or less than others because of your condition.

I carried these beliefs for far too long. It wasn't until I learned to challenge and redefine these labels that I truly began to heal. Breaking free from these imposed identities allowed me to see myself as something much greater: a human being, a fighter, and a survivor.

My Personal Battle with Being Labeled

When I was diagnosed with bipolar disorder, I was relieved to finally have an explanation for my struggles. But that relief quickly turned into something else—a sense of imprisonment. I remember looking at my medical chart and seeing the words "severe mental illness" stamped across the pages. It felt like a life sentence. I began to believe that my future was already written for me, that my worth would forever be tied to my condition. People began treating me differently, even those who loved me. Some approached me with caution, as if I were fragile. Others assumed I was dangerous, unpredictable. Strangers who learned of my diagnosis pitied me, while some kept their distance, as if mental illness were contagious.

But the worst part? I started treating myself differently.

- I stopped believing I could achieve my dreams.
- I began to think of myself as "less than."
- I let my diagnosis dictate what I thought I could or couldn't do.
- I accepted a life of limitations, all because of a label.

For a long time, I let bipolar disorder define me. But one day, I realized something: I am not my diagnosis. Yes, I have bipolar disorder. Yes, it affects my daily life. But it is not the totality of who I am. I am so much more than a label in a medical file. I am a husband, a friend, a speaker, a writer, an advocate, and most of all, a person who has value beyond his struggles.

You are, too.

Shifting from a Victim Mindset to an Empowerment Mindset

Once I realized that labels didn't define me, I had to make a choice: Would I stay in a victim mindset, or would I claim my power? A victim mindset is when we believe that life is happening to us rather than with us. It is when we see ourselves as powerless, controlled by external circumstances. An empowerment mindset is when we take responsibility for our lives, our choices, and our healing. It is when we decide that while we may not control everything that happens to us, we control how we respond.

How I Shifted My Mindset:

1. **Challenging Negative Thoughts**
   - Instead of saying "I am bipolar, so I can't do this," I began saying, "I have bipolar disorder, but I am capable of achieving my goals."
   - Instead of "I am broken," I told myself, "I am healing."
2. **Taking Control of My Narrative**
   - I started sharing my story, not as a tragedy, but as a testimony of resilience.
   - I refused to let others' perceptions of mental illness dictate my identity.
3. **Focusing on Strengths, Not Just Challenges**
   - Yes, I have challenges, but I also have strengths: empathy, perseverance, and the ability to connect with others.
   - Instead of fixating on limitations, I started building on my strengths.
4. **Finding Purpose in My Struggle**
   - I turned my pain into purpose by advocating for mental health awareness.
   - Instead of feeling sorry for myself, I started helping others break free from their own labels.

By shifting from a victim mindset to an empowered mindset, I reclaimed control over my life.

The Role of Language in Shaping Identity

Words shape reality. The language we use can either imprison us or set us free.

For years, I said things like:

- "I am bipolar."
- "I am suicidal."
- "I am mentally ill."

But what if I told you that changing just a few words can change your entire self-perception?

The Power of Language Shift

Instead of saying:

✘ "I am bipolar," try ✓ "I have bipolar disorder."

✘ "I am depressed," try ✓ "I am experiencing depression."

✘ "I am broken," try ✓ "I am healing."

The difference may seem small, but its life changing. Saying "I have" instead of "I am" separates who you are from what you experience. You are not your condition. You are a person who is navigating challenges, but that does not define your identity.

How to Separate Yourself from Your Diagnosis

Separating yourself from a label is not about denial—it's about taking ownership of your identity beyond a diagnosis.

Here's how I learned to break free from the chains of labeling:

1. **Reclaim Your Full Identity**

- Instead of defining myself only by my struggles, I embraced all aspects of who I am—my passions, relationships, and dreams.
- Write down all the things that make you you—your skills, hobbies, relationships, and values. This helps remind you that you are a whole person.

2. **Surround Yourself with the Right People**

- I sought out people who saw me for more than my diagnosis.
- I distanced myself from those who only focused on my struggles and reinforced a limited view of who I was.

3. **Engage in Activities That Reinforce Your Strengths**

- I pursued passions outside of mental health, such as writing, fitness, and storytelling.
- Doing things that made me feel capable reminded me that I was more than my struggles.

4. **Own Your Story—But Don't Let It Own You**

- Your past is part of you, but it doesn't have to define your future.
- You are not your trauma, your mistakes, or your diagnosis.

Moving Forward Without Labels

Breaking free from labels is not a one-time event—it is an ongoing journey. There will be days when you struggle, when old labels creep back in, when you feel defined by your past.

But every day, you have a choice:

- Will you let a label define you?
- Or will you define yourself?

You are more than a diagnosis.

You are more than what others say about you.

You are more than the mistakes of your past.

You are a fighter. A survivor. A human being with unlimited potential.

Choose to see yourself as more than a label. Because you are.

Who Are You Without the Labels?

Take a moment and ask yourself:

- Who am I beyond my diagnosis?
- What strengths do I have that my struggles don't define?
- How can I rewrite my personal narrative to reflect my identity?

Breaking free from labels isn't easy, but it is possible.

And once you do, you'll realize that you were never just a label to begin with—you were always so much more.

Chapter 4:

Building Mental Resilience – How to Turn Struggles into Strength

The Power of Resilience – A Skill, not a Trait

Resilience is not something you are born with. It is not a magical ability given to a select few. Resilience is a skill—a muscle you build through experience, practice, and determination. For a long time, I believed resilience was something I lacked. When I was struggling, I thought I was weak, incapable of overcoming my challenges. But over time, I learned the truth: Resilience is not about never falling—it is about getting back up. This chapter is about building that ability. No matter what you've been through, no matter how many times life has knocked you down, you can become stronger. Science backs it. My life proves it. And by the time you finish this chapter, you'll believe it too.

My Story – Learning Resilience the Hard Way

I know what it feels like to hit rock bottom.

The day I jumped from the Golden Gate Bridge, I thought my life was over. But something happened that I never expected: I survived. When I woke up in the hospital, every bone in my body screamed in pain. My mind was still in turmoil. And yet, something inside me had changed. I had a second chance.

But let's be honest resilience didn't come instantly. It didn't come from simply surviving. It came from what happened afterward.

- It came from facing my pain, instead of running from it.
- It came from asking for help and doing the hard work of recovery.
- It came from choosing, every day, to fight for my mental health.

That choice—to keep going, to keep fighting—is what resilience is all about. And you can make that choice, too.

What Science Says About Resilience

Resilience is not a personality trait. It is a set of behaviors, habits, and thought patterns that anyone can develop.

What makes a person resilient?

Research in psychology and neuroscience has found that resilient people share common traits:

1. **Emotional Regulation** – They can manage their emotions effectively, allowing them to stay calm under stress.
2. **Cognitive Flexibility** – They can adapt and shift perspectives when faced with obstacles.
3. **Optimism with Realism** – They focus on solutions rather than dwelling on problems, but they don't ignore reality.
4. **Social Support** – They surround themselves with people who uplift and encourage them.
5. **Self-Awareness** – They understand their own thoughts, emotions, and reactions.

The Brain and Resilience

- Studies show that the prefrontal cortex (the part of the brain responsible for problem-solving and rational thinking) plays a crucial role in resilience.
- The amygdala (the brain's emotional center) responds to stress, but resilience training can help reduce its overactivity.
- Neuroplasticity—the brain's ability to rewire itself—means that you can train yourself to become more resilient over time.

This means resilience is not something you "either have or don't have." It is something you can build.

Step 1 – Reframing Challenges as Opportunities

One of the most powerful shifts you can make is changing how you see adversity. When I was in the depths of my struggles, I saw every setback as proof that I was failing. But once I began to reframe my struggles, everything changed.

How to Reframe Challenges

1. Instead of "This is happening to me," say "This is happening for me."
   - Every challenge contains an opportunity to learn, grow, and become stronger.
2. Instead of "I can't handle this," say "I am building the strength to handle this."
   - Resilience is built through facing difficulties, not avoiding them.
3. Instead of "This is the end," say "This is a new beginning."
   - Every failure, every mistake, every dark moment is an opportunity to start fresh.

This mental shift is not about ignoring pain—it is about changing your perspective on pain.

Step 2 – The Power of Emotional Regulation

Resilient people don't avoid emotions—they learn how to manage them. For years, I let my emotions control me. When I was sad, I believed it would last forever. When I was anxious, I spiraled into panic. But through therapy and practice, I learned that I could regulate my emotions instead of letting them dictate my life.

How to Regulate Your Emotions

- Pause Before Reacting: Take a deep breath before responding to negative emotions.
- Name Your Emotions: Saying "I feel anxious" or "I feel frustrated" helps you gain control.
- Use Grounding Techniques: Try the 5-4-3-2-1 method—Identify 5 things you see, 4 things you feel, 3 things you hear, 2 things you smell, and 1 thing you taste.
- Practice Mindfulness: Resilient people stay present instead of getting lost in "what ifs."

By regulating your emotions, you gain the power to respond instead of reacting.

Step 3 – Developing Cognitive Flexibility

Cognitive flexibility is the ability to adapt to change and shift your perspective when necessary.

When I was struggling, I had a very rigid way of thinking:

- "Things will never get better."
- "I am always going to feel this way."
- "If something goes wrong, everything is ruined."

This kind of thinking traps you. Resilient people learn to challenge their thoughts and reframe them.

How to Train Cognitive Flexibility:

1. Challenge Absolutes: If you think "I will never be happy," ask yourself: "Has there ever been a time I was happy? What made that possible?"
2. Look for Multiple Solutions: Instead of thinking "I'm stuck," list three possible actions you could take.
3. Practice "Yes, And" Thinking: Instead of "This situation is terrible," try "Yes, this situation is tough, and I can still take steps to improve my life."

This skill frees you from rigid, negative thought patterns.

Step 4 – The Role of Social Support

Resilience is not built alone.

There was a time when I believed asking for help was a weakness. I thought I had to fight my battles in isolation. But the truth is, we need people.

How to Build a Strong Support System:

- Seek People Who Lift You Up: Surround yourself with those who encourage growth.
- Be Open About Your Struggles: Vulnerability creates deeper connections.
- Ask for Help When Needed: It is not weakness; it is strength.

Resilient people don't try to do it all alone. Neither should you.

Step 5 – Creating a Personal Resilience Plan

Now that we've explored the key components of resilience, it's time to build your own Resilience Plan.

Your Personalized Plan:

1. Identify One Challenge You Want to Overcome.
2. Choose One Mindset Shift You Can Make.
3. List Three Coping Strategies to Regulate Emotions.
4. Write Down One Person You Can Reach Out To.
5. Commit to One Daily Habit to Strengthen Resilience.

When you write down your plan, you make it real.

What Happens When You Build Resilience

When you practice resilience daily:

- ✓ You handle stress more effectively.
- ✓ You recover from setbacks faster.
- ✓ You feel more in control of your life.
- ✓ You gain the ability to find meaning in challenges.

Moving Forward with Strength

Resilience is not about avoiding struggles—it is about facing them head-on and growing stronger.

You could turn pain into power. To take hardship and create healing. To become the strongest version of yourself.

And it starts today.

Chapter 5:

The Power of Routine – Structure as a Lifeline

Why Routine Matters for Mental Fitness

When I was at my lowest, my life had no structure. My days felt chaotic, unpredictable, and overwhelming. I woke up with no plan, no direction, and no sense of purpose. Each day blended into the next, and my mind spiraled deeper into darkness.

Then I learned a critical truth: routine is a lifeline.

At first, I resisted it. I thought the structure was rigid, restrictive—something that would make me feel trapped. But I was wrong. I discovered that routine wasn't about control—it was about freedom.

- Freedom from stress, because I knew what to expect.
- Freedom from decision fatigue, because I didn't have to constantly figure out what to do next.
- Freedom from self-doubt, because I was building habits that made me stronger every day.

Science backs this up. Research shows that consistent routines reduce stress, improve mental health, and increase feelings of stability. When you wake up every day with purpose and structure, your mind becomes stronger. This chapter will show you how to create a routine that works for you—one that enhances your mental health, builds resilience, and makes you feel empowered.

My Story – Finding Stability Through Routine

When I was in recovery, my days felt unpredictable. Some days, I had the energy to get out of bed. Other days, I didn't. Some nights, I slept. Others, my thoughts kept me awake for hours. I felt like I was constantly playing defense against my own mind. Then, my therapist gave me an assignment: "Build a simple daily routine and stick to it."

At first, I thought it wouldn't make a difference. But I was desperate to feel better, so I tried it. I started with small changes:

1. Waking up at the same time every morning.
2. Eating breakfast instead of skipping meals.
3. Going for a 10-minute walk each day.
4. Writing one positive thought in a journal.

After a week, something incredible happened. My mind felt clearer. My anxiety lessened. I had fewer emotional crashes. The simple act of creating structure gave me a sense of control over my life.

And it can do the same for you.

The Science Behind Routine and Mental Health

Routines are powerful because they reduce uncertainty and increase stability—two things the brain craves.

How Routine Affects the Brain

- **Reduces Stress:** The brain thrives on predictability. A structured routine lowers cortisol (the stress hormone) and helps prevent mental overload.
- **Improves Sleep:** Going to bed and waking up at the same time regulates your circadian rhythm, making it easier to fall asleep and wake up refreshed.
- **Boosts Mood:** Regular habits, such as exercise and meditation, increase dopamine and serotonin, the brain's "feel-good" chemicals.
- **Strengthens Willpower:** Every decision we make drains mental energy. Routines reduce decision fatigue, freeing up energy for more important tasks.

This means that even the smallest daily habits can have a massive impact on your mental well-being.

Step 1 – The Morning Routine: Start Your Day with Power

How you start your day sets the tone for everything that follows. A chaotic morning leads to a chaotic day. But a structured, intentional morning routine creates momentum and mental clarity.

How to Build a Powerful Morning Routine

1. **Wake Up at the Same Time Every Day** – This regulates your internal clock, reducing fatigue and mental fog.
2. **Hydrate First Thing in the Morning** – Your brain is 75% water; dehydration can lead to poor focus and mood swings.
3. **Avoid Checking Your Phone Immediately** – Scrolling social media floods your brain with distractions and stress before your day has even begun.
4. **Engage in One Mindful Activity** – This could be meditation, journaling, deep breathing, or simply enjoying your coffee in silence.

5. **Move Your Body** – Stretch, take a short walk, or do a quick workout to wake up your nervous system.
6. **Set a Daily Intention** – Ask yourself: What is one thing I want to accomplish today? This creates focus and purpose.

Even if your morning routine only takes 15 minutes, those minutes shape your entire day.

Step 2 – The Power of an Evening Routine

A strong evening routine is just as important as your morning routine. Your nighttime habits determine the quality of your sleep, which directly affects your mental health.

How to Build a Nighttime Routine That Supports Mental Health

1. **Set a Bedtime and Stick to It** – Your brain loves consistency. Going to bed at the same time each night helps regulate your mood and energy levels.
2. **Reduce Screen Time Before Bed** – The blue light from phones and laptops disrupts melatonin production, making it harder to fall asleep.
3. **Create a Wind-Down Ritual** – This could include reading, listening to calming music, or doing light stretching.
4. **Practice Gratitude or Reflection** – Writing down three good things from your day helps shift your focus from stress to appreciation.
5. **Prepare for the Next Day** – Laying out clothes, packing your bag, or writing a to-do list reduces morning stress.

By ending your day with calmness and intention, you set yourself up for success.

Step 3 – Building Micro-Routines for Mental Strength

Routines don't have to be complicated. Some of the most powerful habits take just a few minutes.

Quick Daily Habits That Strengthen Mental Resilience

- The 5-Minute Gratitude Practice – Write down three things you're grateful for.
- Breathing Exercises – Try the 4-7-8 method: Inhale for 4 seconds, hold for 7, exhale for 8.
- The 10-Minute Walk – Walking releases endorphins, reduces stress, and clears your mind.
- Daily Affirmations – Saying, "I am strong, capable, and resilient," rewires your brain for confidence.

Small habits, repeated daily, lead to massive transformations.

Step 4 – Overcoming Resistance to Routine

Creating a new routine is exciting at first, but motivation fades. The key is discipline, not motivation.

How to Stay Consistent with Your Routine

1. Start Small: Don't try to change everything at once. Focus on one habit at a time.
2. Make It Enjoyable: If you hate running, don't force yourself to run—find a workout you enjoy.
3. Track Your Progress: Use a journal or an app to keep yourself accountable.
4. Prepare for Setbacks: If you miss a day, don't quit. Just start again the next day.

Consistency matters more than perfection. Progress is better than all-or-nothing thinking.

The Mindset Shift – Routine Is Self-Care, Not Restriction

Many people resist structure because they see it as restrictive. But routine is not about limitation—it is about liberation. Having a daily structure doesn't mean you're trapping yourself in monotony. It means you are creating a foundation for success.

Reframing Routine as Self-Love

- Instead of "I have to do this," say "I get to do this for my mental health."
- Instead of "Routine is boring," say "Routine creates stability and peace."
- Instead of "I'm bad at sticking to habits," say "I am building habits one step at a time."

Routine is an act of self-care. It is choosing to show up for yourself every day.

Your Personalized Routine Plan

Now, it's time to build your mental wellness routine.

1. Write down one habit you want to start in the morning.
2. Write down one habit you want to add to your nighttime routine.
3. Choose one "micro-routine" to practice daily (breathing, gratitude, journaling, etc.).
4. Commit to consistency.

Even small changes, done consistently, will transform your mental fitness.

Takeaway — Routine is Your Superpower

Creating structure in your life doesn't just help you survive—it helps you thrive. By implementing simple, powerful routines, you build stability, confidence, and control over your mental health. And once you do that, there is nothing you cannot overcome.

Chapter 6:

Nutrition and the Brain – Fueling Mental Health

The Connection Between Food and Mental Health

For years, I thought mental health was only about emotions, therapy, and medication. I never connected what I ate to how I felt. But I was wrong. The day I realized that food directly affects the brain was a game-changer in my mental wellness journey. I used to eat whatever was convenient—fast food, sugar-loaded snacks, and energy drinks to keep myself going. I thought food was just fuel, nothing more. Then, through research and personal experience, I discovered something shocking: the gut and the brain are connected. What I ate either helped me heal or kept me trapped in a cycle of mood swings, fatigue, and mental fog. This chapter is about fueling your brain the right way. If you want to be mentally strong, focused, and resilient, you need to nourish your body and mind.

My Story – How Changing My Diet Changed My Mind

I used to rely on junk food to survive. Sugary cereals in the morning, processed snacks throughout the day, and fast food for dinner. It was quick, easy, and tasted good.

But my mental health was suffering.

- I woke up feeling sluggish and unmotivated.
- I experienced frequent mood swings.
- My anxiety was through the roof.
- I couldn't concentrate for long periods.

At first, I didn't make the connection between my diet and my mental struggles. But when I started working with mental health professionals, one of them asked:

"Kevin, what are you eating? How are you fueling your brain?"

I had never been asked that before. I started tracking my diet, and the results were clear: I was feeding my body garbage, and my mind was paying the price.

So, I made a change.

- I cut back on sugar.
- I started eating whole, natural foods.
- I increased my intake of Omega-3s.
- I drank more water and cut out processed junk.

Within weeks, my energy increased. My mood stabilized. My ability to focus improved. I felt stronger—mentally and physically.

That's when I realized: food is medicine for the brain.

The Science Behind Food and Mental Health

The Gut-Brain Connection

Did you know that 90% of serotonin (the "happiness chemical") is produced in your gut? The gut and brain communicate through the vagus nerve, meaning that what you eat directly impacts your mood, emotions, and cognitive function. When your gut is inflamed or imbalanced, your brain feels the effects—leading to increased anxiety, depression, and brain fog.

Nutrients That Fuel Mental Health

Research has shown that specific nutrients boost brain function and help regulate mood:

1. Omega-3 Fatty Acids – Found in salmon, walnuts, and flaxseeds. These help fight depression and improve focus.
2. Magnesium – Found in spinach, almonds, and bananas. This helps reduce anxiety and promote relaxation.
3. B Vitamins – Found in eggs, whole grains, and leafy greens. They play a critical role in energy production and mood stability.
4. Probiotics – Found in yogurt, kimchi, and sauerkraut. These help balance gut bacteria, which improves brain function.

When you fuel your body with the right nutrients, your brain thrives.

The Foods That Are Destroying Your Mental Health

Just as some foods fuel the brain, others damage it.

Foods That Harm Mental Health:

✖ Refined Sugars & Processed Carbs

- Cause blood sugar spikes and crashes, leading to mood swings and energy dips.
- Linked to increased risk of depression.

✖ Artificial Sweeteners

- Some, like aspartame, can disrupt neurotransmitter function and increase anxiety.

✖ Trans Fats & Processed Oils

- Found in fried foods, margarine, and packaged snacks. Cause inflammation in the brain, leading to cognitive decline.

✖ Excessive Caffeine & Energy Drinks

- Can increase anxiety and disrupt sleep, which affects mental clarity.

When I cut these out, I noticed an immediate difference in my mental clarity, emotional stability, and energy levels.

Step 1 – Start with Hydration

Before changing anything else, start by drinking more water.

Dehydration can cause:

- Fatigue
- Brain fog
- Irritability
- Increased anxiety

I used to drink sodas and coffee all day, thinking I was staying hydrated. But when I switched to pure water, I felt more alert, my headaches went away, and my mood stabilized.

Action Step:

- Start your day with a full glass of water.
- Carry a water bottle and sip throughout the day.
- Reduce sodas and energy drinks—they dehydrate you.

Water is the simplest yet most overlooked mental health tool.

Step 2 – Balance Your Blood Sugar

Your brain needs steady energy to function.

When your blood sugar spikes (from eating junk food), your energy goes up temporarily—but then crashes. This rollercoaster effect leads to mood swings, irritability, and brain fog.

How to Keep Blood Sugar Stable:

- ✓ Eat protein with every meal (chicken, fish, tofu, beans).
- ✓ Choose complex carbs over simple ones (quinoa, brown rice, whole oats).
- ✓ Avoid excess sugar and processed foods.
- ✓ Eat healthy fats (avocados, nuts, olive oil) to slow digestion and keep energy stable.

This simple shift can dramatically improve mood and focus.

Step 3 – Eat for Brainpower

The Mental Health Superfoods:

🥑 Avocados – High in healthy fats that support brain function.

🫐 Berries – Rich in antioxidants that protect the brain.

🥚 Eggs – Full of choline, which helps with memory.

🌿 Leafy Greens – Provide essential nutrients like folate and iron.

🐟 Fatty Fish (Salmon, Tuna) – Packed with Omega-3s for mood stability.

When I started adding these to my meals, I felt the difference.

Step 4 – The 80/20 Rule

Let's be real—you don't have to eat "perfectly" to see benefits.

I follow the 80/20 rule:

☑ 80% of the time, I eat whole, nutrient-dense foods.

🍕 20% of the time, I allow myself treats without guilt.

This balance prevents restriction, obsession, and burnout. Mental wellness is about sustainability, not perfection.

Creating Your Personalized Brain-Boosting Meal Plan

Now it's time to create your own mental wellness meal plan.

Step 1 – Identify One Small Change You Can Make Today

📌 Swap soda for water.

📌 Add one serving of vegetables to your meals.

📌 Replace processed snacks with nuts or fruit.

Step 2 – Plan One Brain-Boosting Meal Per Day

🍳 Example:

- **Breakfast:** Scrambled eggs with avocado
- **Lunch:** Grilled chicken with spinach salad
- **Dinner:** Salmon with quinoa and roasted veggies

The goal is progress, not perfection.

Food Is Medicine for the Mind

Your brain is either being fueled or being harmed by what you eat.

- Eat whole, nutrient-dense foods.
- Stay hydrated.
- Avoid processed junk that causes inflammation.
- Create a sustainable, balanced eating pattern.

The right nutrition won't just make you feel better physically—it will transform your mental health.

Because when you fuel your body, you fuel your mind.

Chapter 7:

Exercise for the Mind and Body – Moving Toward Wellness

Why Movement Matters for Mental Health

For years, I thought exercise was only about looking good, building muscle, or losing weight. I never connected movement with mental health. I didn't realize that exercise is medicine for the brain. I didn't know that movement could be the difference between sinking into depression or pulling myself out of it. I know what it's like to be in unbearable brain pain. I have lived with bipolar disorder, suicidal ideation, and the relentless battle between my mind and my will to live. I know what it feels like to believe there is no way out.

But here's what I also know: suicide is not the answer. It is the problem. What changed my life—what kept me alive when my mind tried to convince me otherwise—was taking action, even when I didn't feel like it. And one of the most powerful actions I took was moving my body. This chapter isn't about running marathons or lifting heavy weights. It's about using movement as a tool to heal your mind, to fight for your life, and to build resilience that will carry you through the hardest days. Because if you are moving, you are still here. And if you are still here, you can survive.

My Story – Living with Bipolar Disorder and Finding Strength Through Movement

I have bipolar disorder. That is a fact.

It means my brain does not always cooperate. It means I have days where I feel unstoppable and days where I feel like I am drowning in darkness. It means I have faced suicidal ideation more times than I can count. It means that on September 25, 2000, I jumped off the Golden Gate Bridge. I believed in that moment that my pain was permanent. I thought I was a burden. I thought I had no way out. The second my hands left the rail, I knew I had made a mistake. I survived that day, but survival wasn't just about the fact that I lived. Survival became a choice I had to make every single day after that. One of the ways I fought for my life was through movement. At first, it wasn't about fitness—it was about getting out of my head.

I started small:

- A walk when my thoughts became overwhelming.
- Push-ups when I felt my emotions spiraling.
- Stretching when anxiety gripped my chest.

Every time I moved, I reminded myself: I am alive. I am here. I am choosing to fight. That choice—made repeatedly—built a new kind of resilience. Movement became my therapy, my anchor, and my proof that I was stronger than the voice in my head telling me to give up.

Brain Pain vs. Mental Pain – A New Perspective on Mental Health

We need to change the way we talk about mental health. For too long, we have used language that carries shame, stigma, and negativity. The term "mental illness" often makes people feel broken, as if something is wrong with them.

But what if we reframed it?

Brain Pain vs. Mental Pain

- If you break your arm, you don't feel "bone weakness"—you feel bone pain.
- If you have a heart problem, you don't say you have "mental heart illness"—you say you have heart disease.
- If you struggle with depression, anxiety, or bipolar disorder, it's not a "mental weakness"—it's brain pain.

Your brain is an organ, just like your heart and your lungs. And just like any other organ, it can be injured, or diseased. It can heal, and it needs care. When I started seeing my struggles as brain pain rather than a personal flaw, it changed everything. It meant I wasn't weak—I was healing. It meant I didn't have to be ashamed—I had to find solutions.

And one of the most powerful solutions was movement.

The Science of Exercise and Brain Health

Exercise doesn't just change your body. It changes your brain.

How Exercise Heals the Brain

◉ **Increases Neuroplasticity** – Movement helps the brain grow new neural connections, making it more adaptable and resilient.

⚡ **Boosts Dopamine & Serotonin** – Exercise naturally increases the "feel-good" chemicals in your brain, which help regulate mood.

◉ **Reduces Stress Hormones** – Movement lowers cortisol levels, reducing feelings of anxiety and tension.

😴 **Improves Sleep** – Regular exercise helps regulate sleep cycles, making it easier to fall and stay asleep.

💡 **Enhances Focus & Memory** – Aerobic activity increases blood flow to the brain, improving cognitive function.

This means that exercise isn't just good for your body—it is critical for your brain.

Step 1 – Moving Through Depression and Suicidal Thoughts

I know how hard it is to move when you feel like you can't. When depression hits, it tells you to stay in bed, isolate yourself, and shut down. But action—any action—is the enemy of depression.

How to Move When You Don't Want To

- **Start Small:** Walk to the mailbox. Stretch for two minutes. Do one jumping jack.
- **Make it a Ritual:** Schedule movement like a daily appointment with yourself.
- **Connect It to Something You Love:** Dance to music, walk in nature, play with your pet.
- **Remind Yourself of the Goal:** You're not moving to "look better"—you're moving to feel better.

The hardest part is starting. But once you move, the momentum builds.

Step 2 – Finding the Right Kind of Movement for You

You don't need to run marathons. You don't need to lift heavy weights.

You just need to move.

Different Forms of Movement for Mental Health

🧘 **Yoga** – Helps with anxiety, stress relief, and body awareness.

🏃 **Running or Walking** – Clears the mind and releases endorphins.

🥊 **Martial Arts or Boxing** – Provides a healthy outlet for frustration and stress.

🚴 **Cycling or Swimming** – Combines physical exertion with mindfulness.

🏋 **Strength Training** – Builds confidence and resilience.

Find what works for you. The best exercise is the one you'll actually do.

Step 3 – Movement as a Daily Habit

To make movement part of your mental health routine:

- ✓ Schedule it like an appointment.
- ✓ Make it easy and accessible.
- ✓ Track your progress and celebrate small wins.
- ✓ Find a workout partner for accountability.

Small, consistent action leads to massive transformation.

Step 4 – How Exercise Saved My Life

Exercise is not just about physical health.

It is about fighting back against the darkness.

It is about proving to yourself every day that you are still here, still fighting, still choosing to live.

Every time I move, I remind myself:

- I am alive.
- I am stronger than my brain pain.
- I am fighting, and I will never stop.

Your Personal Movement Plan

☑ What is one small movement you can start today?

☑ How can you make exercise part of your routine?

☑ Who can you ask to support your movement journey?

Write it down. Commit to it. This is your fight. And movement is your weapon.

Keep Moving, Keep Living

If you are moving, you are still here.

If you are still here, you can survive.

And if you can survive, you can thrive.

Keep moving. Keep fighting. Keep living.

Chapter 8:

Sleep as Medicine – Restoring the Mind

The Missing Piece in Mental Health – Sleep

For years, I battled bipolar disorder, depression, and suicidal ideation without realizing that one of the most powerful tools for managing my brain pain was something I had ignored my entire life: sleep. I used to think sleep was optional. I believed that if I just worked harder, pushed through the exhaustion, and ignored the fatigue, I would eventually "fix" my mental health. I was wrong. Sleep is not a luxury. It is not something you can just "catch up on" later. It is medicine for the brain. It is the foundation of mental wellness. Without it, everything else—therapy, exercise, nutrition, medication—becomes less effective. This chapter is about understanding why sleep is essential, how I changed my relationship with rest, and how you can use sleep as a tool to heal, strengthen, and transform your mind.

My Story – How Sleep (Or the Lack of It) Affected My Mental Health

For most of my life, my sleep was a disaster.

- I stayed up late scrolling, worrying, or replaying every mistake I had ever made.
- I would wake up multiple times a night, my mind racing.
- Some nights, I barely slept at all.
- Other times, I would sleep 14+ hours and still feel exhausted.

I didn't know that poor sleep was fueling my bipolar disorder, increasing my mood swings, and making my suicidal thoughts worse. In 2000, when I attempted to take my life by jumping from the Golden Gate Bridge, my sleep was at its worst. I was running on empty—mentally, emotionally, and physically. After I survived, I knew I had to change everything about my life. One of the first things I fixed was my sleep. When I started prioritizing rest, my life changed. My mood became more stable. My thinking became clearer. My emotions became easier to manage.

Now, I see sleep as a non-negotiable part of my mental health plan.

The Science of Sleep and Brain Health

What Happens to the Brain During Sleep?

1. **Emotional Processing** – Your brain sorts through emotions, making it easier to regulate mood.
2. **Memory Consolidation** – Sleep strengthens learning and memory retention.
3. **Detoxification** – The brain flushes out toxins linked to neurological diseases.
4. **Hormone Regulation** – Proper sleep balances cortisol (stress hormone) and serotonin (happiness chemical).

How Poor Sleep Impacts Mental Health

🔔 Increases anxiety and depression

🔔 Worsens mood swings (especially for bipolar disorder)

🔔 Weakens impulse control (increasing risk of self-harm)

🔔 Impairs problem-solving and decision-making

When you don't get enough sleep, your brain struggles to function. It's like trying to drive a car without gas. You can't heal, think, or thrive without rest.

Step 1 – Fixing My Sleep, Fixing My Life

I didn't fix my sleep overnight, but once I committed to consistent, high-quality rest, I saw massive improvements.

What I Changed:

- ✓ Set a consistent bedtime and wake-up time (even on weekends).
- ✓ Stopped using my phone before bed—no more late-night doom-scrolling.
- ✓ Created a calming pre-bedtime routine (reading, deep breathing, light stretching).
- ✓ Used blackout curtains to make my room completely dark.
- ✓ Avoid caffeine late in the day.

Within weeks, I felt more energetic, more stable, and more in control of my emotions. Sleep became a form of self-respect and self-care.

Step 2 – The Hero's Perspective Shift

- For years, I saw myself as a victim of my bipolar disorder.
- I believed that my struggles would always define me.
- I believed that I would never escape the brain pain.
- But over time, I learned that I was not the victim—I was the hero.

How I Changed My Perspective:

1. Instead of "I suffer from bipolar disorder," I said, "I live with bipolar disorder, and I fight every day."
2. Instead of "I am broken," I said, "I am healing."
3. Instead of "My past defines me," I said, "I define my future."

Becoming the hero of my own story meant taking ownership of my mental health. Fixing my sleep was part of that journey.

And once I did, everything else—my happiness, my relationships, my purpose—began to fall into place.

The Things I Would Have Missed

If I had died by suicide in 2000, I would have missed everything that makes my life beautiful today.

- I would have missed meeting the love of my life, Margaret Hines.
- I would have missed the joy of sharing my story and helping others heal.
- I would have missed the moments of laughter, of deep conversations, of quiet sunsets.
- I would have missed proving to myself that I could survive and thrive.

When I think back to that moment on the bridge, I wish I could tell my younger self:

"Hold on. You have no idea how beautiful life is going to be."

And now, I say that same message to you.

Step 3 – Creating Your Personal Sleep Routine

🛏 Set a bedtime and stick to it.

🚫 Put your phone away 30 minutes before bed.

🌙 Make your bedroom dark and cool.

📖 Do a relaxing activity before sleep (reading, meditating, journaling).

🚶 Get sunlight and movement during the day to regulate your sleep cycle.

If you struggle with mental health, fixing your sleep is one of the most powerful things you can do.

The Future You Deserve

If you are struggling right now, please hear this:

You have a future worth fighting for.

- You will love and be loved.
- You will experience joy you never thought possible.
- You will become stronger than you ever imagined.

You don't need to be perfect. You just need to keep going.

Keep Fighting, Keep Living

I almost didn't get to live this life.

I almost didn't get to know the joy of waking up next to Margaret every morning.

I almost didn't get to experience the beauty of helping others through their pain.

I almost didn't get to prove to myself that I am so much more than my brain pain.

But I did.

And so will you.

Your story is still being written. Keep writing.

What You Can Do Today

♥ Commit to improving your sleep starting tonight.

♥ Shift your perspective from victim to hero.

♥ Remind yourself of all the things you will experience in the future.

♥ Know that your pain is temporary, but your impact can be permanent.

You are alive. You are here. You are meant to be.

Chapter 9:

Mindfulness and Meditation – Learning to Be Present

The Power of Presence

For much of my life, I lived in two places: the past and the future.

- I replayed my mistakes over and over in my mind.
- I worried endlessly about what would happen next.
- I lived with bipolar disorder, which meant my brain often felt like a war zone—constant highs and devastating lows.

I was everywhere except the only place that truly mattered: the present moment. After my suicide attempt in 2000, I started searching for ways to heal. Therapy, medication, nutrition, and exercise all played a role in my recovery. But there was one tool that completely changed my relationship with my mind: mindfulness. This chapter is about how learning to be present saved my life, and how you can use mindfulness and meditation to calm your brain, reduce your suffering, and reconnect with the beauty of being alive.

My Story – The Battle with My Own Mind

I remember what it felt like to have a mind that refused to quiet down.

- My manic episodes made my thoughts race like a runaway train.
- My depressive episodes made my mind feel like an anchor, pulling me into the depths.
- My suicidal ideation convinced me that I had no future, no way out.

I couldn't focus. I couldn't slow down. I couldn't find peace.

I thought my brain was my enemy—until I learned how to work with it instead of against it.

I discovered mindfulness, and for the first time, I understood:

- I am not my thoughts.
- My thoughts do not have to become my actions.
- My thoughts can simply be my thoughts.
- They don't have to own, rule, or define me.
- I can always ask for help.
- I am not my past.
- I am not my pain.
- I am simply here. Alive. Breathing. In this moment.

This realization changed everything.

What Is Mindfulness?

Mindfulness is the practice of being fully present, aware, and engaged in the current moment—without judgment.

It means:

- ✓ Letting go of the past and not obsessing over the future.

- ✓ Observing your thoughts without letting them control you.

- ✓ Experiencing life as it is, rather than how you fear it might be.

For people living with brain pain, mindfulness is one of the most powerful tools for calming an overactive mind. It's not about stopping your thoughts. It's about changing your relationship with them.

The Science of Mindfulness and the Brain

Studies have shown that mindfulness literally changes the brain.

How Mindfulness Heals the Mind

🧠 **Reduces Anxiety & Depression** – Lowers activity in the amygdala (fear center) and increases emotional regulation.

⬣ **Decreases Overthinking** – Strengthens the prefrontal cortex, which helps with focus and decision-making.

👤 **Increases Feel-Good Chemicals** – Boosts serotonin and dopamine, which help stabilize mood.

💡 **Creates Mental Clarity** – Helps people with bipolar disorder regulate their thoughts.

When you practice mindfulness, you rewire your brain to be more peaceful, focused, and resilient.

Step 1 – The Power of Breathing

When I first learned mindfulness, my therapist told me:

"Kevin, just breathe."

At first, it sounded ridiculous. How could breathing help my mind?

Then I tried it.

The 4-7-8 Breathing Method

1. Inhale deeply through your nose for 4 seconds.
2. Hold your breath for 7 seconds.
3. Exhale slowly through your mouth for 8 seconds.

After just a few rounds, I felt calmer. My thoughts slowed. My anxiety lessened. I realized that when I focused on my breath, I couldn't focus on my fears at the same time. Breathing became my anchor. No matter how loud my thoughts got, my breath was always there to bring me back. I maintained focused breathing every morning, afternoon, and evening. Before every keynote, during every anxiety attack. I use it daily to keep me balanced, and in the moment.

Step 2 – Learning to Observe Your Thoughts

I used to believe everything my brain told me.

- "You're not good enough."
- "You will never get better."
- "No one truly cares about you."

These thoughts felt real. But mindfulness taught me something crucial:

Thoughts are not facts.

Mindfulness Exercise: The Thought Train

Imagine your thoughts as trains passing by.

- Instead of jumping on every train, just watch them go by.
- If a thought says, "I'm worthless," you don't have to believe it—you can simply let it pass.
- If a thought says, "This feeling will never end," remind yourself: Every feeling is temporary.

This simple shift—observing instead of reacting—can be life-changing.

Step 3 – The Art of Gratitude and Presence

When I was struggling, I spent so much time focusing on what I had lost—my sense of control, my peace, my confidence.

Mindfulness helped me start focusing on what I still had.

- I had my breath.
- I had my heartbeat.
- I had this moment.

Daily Gratitude Practice

Every morning, write down three things you are grateful for. Even if it's small—"I'm grateful for sunlight," "I'm grateful for my dog," *"I'm grateful for coffee"—it shifts your perspective. Gratitude is one of the fastest ways to bring yourself back into the present moment.

What I Would Have Missed If I Had Died in 2000

If I had died by suicide, I would have missed everything that makes my life beautiful today.

- I would have missed Margaret, the love of my life.
- I would have missed laughing with friends, sharing my story, and helping others heal.
- I would have missed proving to myself that I am stronger than my brain pain.

I almost let my thoughts convince me that I had no future.

But my thoughts were wrong.

And if you are struggling right now, I need you to hear this:

Your thoughts are not your truth.

Your pain is temporary.

Your life is worth fighting for.

Your Personal Mindfulness Plan

Mindfulness is a practice, not a destination. Start small.

- ✓ Try 1 minute of deep breathing today.
- ✓ Write down 3 things you're grateful for.
- ✓ Go for a short walk and focus only on your surroundings.
- ✓ When a negative thought appears, simply observe it—don't fight it.

These small habits can change your brain and save your life.

The Present Moment Is Enough

I spent too much of my life trapped in the past and fearing the future.

Mindfulness taught me this: The only moment that truly exists is now.

And right now,

You are here.

You are breathing.

You are alive.

That is enough.

Keep choosing to be present. Keep choosing to stay.

Because the future you can't see yet? It is worth it.

Chapter 10:

Emotional Intelligence – Understanding and Controlling Your Emotions

Why Emotional Intelligence Is the Key to Mental Strength

For much of my life, I thought my emotions controlled me.

- When I was manic, I felt invincible. I made impulsive decisions, said things I didn't mean, and felt like I was on top of the world—until I wasn't.
- When I was depressed, I felt like I was drowning. Every little thing overwhelmed me, and I believed the pain would never end.
- When I was suicidal, I was convinced my feelings were facts. My mind told me I was a burden, that I had no future, that I was trapped.

But I was wrong.

My emotions weren't the problem—my lack of understanding and control over them was. That's where emotional intelligence comes in. Emotional intelligence (EI) is the ability to recognize, understand, and manage your emotions in a way that benefits your life. It's the difference between reacting and responding. Between spiraling and staying steady. Between making decisions from pain and making them from wisdom. This chapter is about learning how to master your emotions, so they don't master you.

My Story – How Unchecked Emotions Nearly Took My Life

I remember the day I jumped off the Golden Gate Bridge.

In that moment, I wasn't thinking rationally.

I wasn't weighing the pros and cons.

I wasn't seeing the bigger picture.

I was drowning in emotion.

At that time, I didn't know how to manage my brain pain. I let my feelings dictate my actions. I believed the hopelessness I felt was permanent when it was temporary. I didn't need to die. I needed a new way to deal with my emotions.

Fast forward to today, and my life is filled with purpose, joy, and love.

- I am happily married to Margaret, the love of my life.
- I travel the world, sharing my story and helping others.
- I wake up grateful every single day that I am still here.

I almost didn't get to see any of this—because I let my emotions take control instead of learning how to manage them. Now, I understand: Feelings are powerful, but they don't have to control you.

What Is Emotional Intelligence?

Emotional intelligence is made up of four key skills:

1. **Self-Awareness** – Understanding your emotions and what triggers them.
2. **Self-Regulation** – Managing your emotions in a way that helps, rather than harms.
3. **Social Awareness** – Recognizing emotions in others and responding with empathy.
4. **Relationship Management** – Using emotional intelligence to build stronger, healthier connections.

When you build emotional intelligence, you gain power over your own mind. You stop reacting impulsively. You stop making decisions from a place of fear. You learn to pause, reflect, and choose your response.

This one skill can transform every aspect of your life.

Step 1 – Becoming Aware of Your Emotions

Before you can control your emotions, you must understand them.

Mindfulness Exercise: Name It to Tame It

The next time you feel overwhelmed, try this:

1. Pause. Instead of reacting, take a deep breath.
2. Name your emotion. Say it out loud: "I feel anxious. I feel frustrated. I feel sad."
3. Ask yourself why. What triggered this emotion? Is it tied to something deeper?
4. Remind yourself that emotions pass. Just like clouds in the sky, emotions are temporary.

By identifying your emotions, you take away their power. You shift from being controlled by your feelings to understanding them.

Step 2 – Learning to Regulate Your Emotions

When I was younger, my emotions felt like tsunamis.

When I was happy, I was too happy—manic, impulsive, reckless.

When I was sad, I was too sad—hopeless, withdrawn, drowning.

I had no middle ground. No balance. No emotional regulation.

How I Learned to Manage My Emotions

- ✓ I practiced deep breathing – When my emotions ran high, I used the 4-7-8 method to calm my nervous system.
- ✓ I changed my self-talk – Instead of saying, "I can't handle this," I said, "I can get through this moment."
- ✓ I created a "pause rule" – Before reacting, I took 10 seconds to breathe, assess, and choose my response.
- ✓ I journaled my emotions – Writing helped me process my feelings instead of being overwhelmed by them.

Regulating emotions isn't about suppressing them. It's about learning how to experience them without letting them control you.

Step 3 – Reframing Negative Emotions

For a long time, I saw my bipolar disorder as a curse. I resented my brain pain. I wished I could be "normal."

Then, I changed my perspective.

I started asking:

- "What if my emotions aren't my enemy?"
- "What if my deep sensitivity allows me to connect with others?"
- "What if my struggles are part of my purpose?"

This shift changed everything.

Your emotions are not the enemy. They are information.

Instead of fighting your emotions, listen to what they're telling you.

- Anxiety? It's telling you to prepare, but not to panic.
- Sadness? It's reminding you that something needs attention.
- Anger? It's highlighting an injustice or a boundary that needs to be set.

When you reframe emotions as teachers rather than threats, you gain control.

Step 4 – Understanding Other People's Emotions

Emotional intelligence isn't just about your own feelings—it's about understanding others.

Before I built emotional intelligence, I reacted to people without thinking.

- If someone upset me, I lashed out.
- If someone misunderstood me, I took it personally.
- If someone was struggling, I didn't always recognize it.

Now, I practice social awareness.

How to Improve Your Social Awareness

- ✓ Observe, don't assume. Instead of jumping to conclusions, ask yourself, "What might this person be going through?"
- ✓ Listen to understand, not to respond. Most people just want to be heard.
- ✓ Respond with empathy. Sometimes, the best thing you can say is, "I see you. I hear you. I'm here for you."

The better you understand emotions—your own and others'—the stronger your relationships will be.

The Life I Almost Missed – And Why Emotional Intelligence Saved Me

If I had died in 2000, I would have missed everything.

- I would have missed meeting Margaret, my best friend, my partner, my everything.
- I would have missed the chance to share my story and help others heal.
- I would have missed the realization that my brain pain does not define me.

I almost let my emotions control my fate.

But I didn't.

Because I learned that emotions—even the darkest, heaviest ones—are temporary. And if you can sit with them, process them, and understand them, you will always make it through.

Your Emotional Intelligence Action Plan

📝 Write down three emotions you've struggled with lately.

🧘 Practice deep breathing when those emotions arise.

💡 Reframe one negative emotion as a message instead of a threat.

👂 Practice listening to others with empathy this week.

The more you practice, the stronger your emotional intelligence will become.

Master Your Emotions, Master Your Life

Emotions are not your enemy.

They do not define you.

They are not permanent.

But your ability to manage them? That changes everything.

Master your emotions, and you master your mind.

Master your mind, and you master your life.

And when you master your life, you don't just survive—you thrive.

Chapter 11:

The Role of Social Connection – Why We Need Each Other

The Power of Human Connection

For years, I thought I could fight my battles alone.

I believed that if I just worked harder, pushed through the pain, and kept everything inside, I could somehow "fix" myself.

But I was wrong.

The truth is, we are not meant to do this alone.

- We heal through connection.
- We grow through relationships.
- We find strength in the people who remind us that we are not alone.

When I was at my lowest—living with bipolar disorder, battling suicidal ideation, and drowning in brain pain—I didn't see a way out. But what saved me wasn't just therapy, medication, or even my own willpower. It was people. This chapter is about the life-changing power of human connection and why we all need a support system, a tribe, a community.

Because the people around us can either save us or isolate us. And when we build strong, healthy relationships, we create a foundation for lasting mental wellness.

My Story – The Moment I Realized I Needed People

After I survived jumping from the Golden Gate Bridge, I faced a long and painful recovery—not just physically, but emotionally. I wanted to believe I could handle it all myself. I told myself, "You've survived the impossible—just keep going." But surviving isn't the same as healing. And healing requires other people. I remember the moment everything changed. I was sitting alone, feeling exhausted by my own thoughts, when a simple question hit me:

"What if I let people help me?"

I started talking. Sharing my struggles. Opening up. And everything shifted.

- My therapist became my guide.
- My family became my safety net.
- My wife, Margaret, became my anchor—the love I never thought I would get to experience.

I learned that vulnerability is not weakness—it is strength. And when I allowed myself to be seen, supported, and loved, I truly began to heal.

Why We Need Each Other – The Science of Connection

Human connection isn't just nice to have—it's a biological necessity. Studies show that social connection is one of the biggest predictors of long-term mental health.

People with strong relationships:

- ✅ Experience less depression and anxiety

- ✅ Have stronger immune systems

- ✅ Recover faster from illness and trauma

- ✅ Live longer, happier lives

Why? Because our brains are wired for connection.

When we connect with others, our brains release oxytocin, the "bonding hormone." It lowers stress, calms the nervous system, and strengthens emotional resilience. Loneliness, on the other hand, is as dangerous as smoking 15 cigarettes a day. It increases the risk of depression, heart disease, and even early death.

This means that connection isn't just a feel-good thing—it's a life-saving thing.

Step 1 – Recognizing Toxic Isolation vs. Healthy Solitude

There is a big difference between healthy solitude and toxic isolation.

Healthy Solitude:

- ✅ Taking time to recharge and reflect

- ✅ Engaging in solo activities that bring you peace (journaling, meditating, exercising)

- ✅ Enjoying your own company without feeling lonely

Toxic Isolation:

✖ Avoiding people because of shame or fear

✖ Thinking, "No one understands me, so what's the point?"

✖ Letting loneliness convince you that you are better off alone

When I was at my lowest, I didn't want to be around anyone. I convinced myself that no one could possibly understand my pain. But that was the brain pain talking—it was a lie. The truth is, the more we pull away, the worse we feel. Connection is the antidote.

Step 2 – Finding Your Support System

Not everyone deserves a front-row seat in your life. But everyone deserves a tribe.

Who Should Be in Your Support System?

☑ People who listen without judgment

☑ People who uplift you, not drain you

☑ People who show up for you when you need them most

☑ People who remind you of your worth, even when you forget

I found my support system in many places:

- My wife, Margaret, who loves me unconditionally.
- My friends and family, who stand by me no matter what.
- My therapist, who gives me tools to navigate my mind.
- My mental health community, who remind me I'm not alone.

How to Build Your Support System:

- ✓ Start by identifying one person you trust.
- ✓ Join a support group, online or in person.
- ✓ Be open about your struggles—it invites real connection.
- ✓ Cut ties with people who make you feel worse.

Having the right people in your life can be the difference between sinking and staying afloat.

Step 3 – How to Ask for Help (Without Feeling Like a Burden)

One of the biggest lies brain-pain tells us is:

"If you ask for help, you're a burden."

Let me tell you right now: That is NOT true.

When I finally started asking for help, I realized something: The people who love you WANT to help. They just don't always know how.

How to Ask for Support:

1. Be Honest: "I'm struggling, and I don't know what to do."
2. Be Specific: "Can we talk? I just need someone to listen."
3. Don't Apologize for Needing Help: You are not a burden. You are a human being, and we all need support.

Asking for help is not weakness—it is COURAGE.

Step 4 – Giving Back: The Healing Power of Helping Others

The more I healed, the more I realized something powerful:

Helping others is one of the greatest forms of self-healing.

When I share my story, when I listen to someone struggling, when I remind another person that they are not alone—I heal, too.

How to Give Back Without Overextending Yourself:

- ✓ Be there for a friend in need
- ✓ Volunteer in a cause that matters to you
- ✓ Join a mental health advocacy group
- ✓ Share your story—it might save a life

Healing isn't just about receiving support—it's also about giving it.

The Life I Almost Missed – And the Love I Found

If I had died by suicide in 2000, I would have missed everything.

- I would have missed falling in love with Margaret, the woman who changed my life.
- I would have missed the friendships that make my world brighter.
- I would have missed every hug, every laugh, every late-night conversation.
- I would have missed proving to myself that I am stronger than my pain.

I almost let my brain pain convince me that I was alone.

But I wasn't.

And neither are you.

Your Connection Action Plan

♥ Reach out to ONE person today—just to check in.

♥ Write down three people who support you.

♥ If you feel isolated, take one small step to build your tribe.

🖤 Remind yourself: Connection is not a luxury—it is a necessity.

You Are Not Alone

I have learned many things on my journey, but this might be the most important:

You are not meant to do this alone.

There are people who love you.

There are people who will show up for you.

There are people who need you just as much as you need them.

Let them in.

Let yourself be seen.

Let yourself be loved.

Because life is too beautiful to go through it alone.

Chapter 12:

The Art of Letting Go – Releasing What No Longer Serves You

Why Letting Go Is the Hardest and Most Powerful Thing You'll Ever Do

If I could go back and tell my younger self one thing, it would be this:

"Kevin, you are carrying too much."

- Too much guilt.
- Too much pain.
- Too many memories of moments you wish you could change.

For years, I held onto every mistake, every wrong turn, every regret.

I carried the weight of my past, and it nearly destroyed me.

But here's what I have learned:

We cannot move forward while holding onto what is dragging us down.

Letting go is not about forgetting.

It's not about pretending the past never happened.

It's about freeing yourself from the things that no longer serve you.

Because when you let go, you don't just lose the weight—you gain the space to grow.

My Story – The Burden I Didn't Know I Was Carrying

After I survived jumping from the Golden Gate Bridge, I thought I had been given a second chance at life. But what I didn't realize was that surviving is not the same as healing.

I was alive, but I was still drowning in:

- Shame. For the pain I had caused my family.
- Guilt. For believing I had let people down.
- Anger. At myself for thinking death was the only way out.

For years, I clung to these emotions like I deserved them—like punishing myself was the only way to atone for the past.

But one day, my therapist asked me:

"Kevin, what would happen if you forgave yourself?"

At first, I rejected the idea. Forgive myself? No. I didn't deserve that.

But then I realized something:

Holding onto guilt was not making me a better person.

Holding onto shame was not changing the past.

Holding onto pain was only keeping me from the life I was meant to live.

And at that moment, I made a choice: I would learn to let go.

The Truth About Letting Go

Most people think letting go means:

- Forgetting what happened.
- Pretending it didn't hurt.
- Acting like it doesn't matter.

But that's not true.

Letting go is not about erasing the past.

It's about choosing not to let it control you anymore.

- You can remember what happened without reliving the pain.
- You can acknowledge the past without letting it define your future.
- You can hold onto lessons but release the suffering.

Letting go is not weakness.

It is the ultimate strength.

Because the hardest thing in the world is to say:

"I am done carrying this."

Step 1 – Identifying What's Holding You Back

Take a moment and ask yourself:

"What am I still holding onto that is weighing me down?"

It might be:

- A painful memory
- A toxic relationship

- A mistake from the past
- A belief about yourself that is no longer true

Write it down. Name it. Bring it into the light.

Because the first step in letting go is recognizing what needs to be released.

Step 2 – Understanding Why We Struggle to Let Go

If letting go is so freeing, why is it so hard?

Because we become attached to our pain.

- Guilt can feel like atonement. (If I let go, does that mean I don't care?)
- Anger can feel like protection. (If I let go, does that mean they win?)
- Pain can feel like identity. (If I let go, who am I without this?)

But here's the truth:

- Letting go does not mean you don't care.
- Letting go does not mean you are weak.
- Letting go does not mean forgetting—it means freeing yourself.

It means saying:

"I deserve peace."

And you do.

Step 3 – Practicing Forgiveness (Including Self-Forgiveness)

Forgiveness is one of the most powerful forms of letting go.

- Forgiving others is about releasing the hold they have over you.
- Forgiving yourself is about accepting that you are human, and humans make mistakes.

How to Start Forgiving:

1. Acknowledge the pain. Don't suppress it—face it.
2. Shift your perspective. What can this experience teach you?
3. Decide to release it. You may not feel ready, but the decision comes first.
4. Repeat the process. Forgiveness is a journey, not a one-time event.

You don't forgive for them. You forgive for you.

Step 4 – Releasing the Need for Control

Sometimes, what we need to let go of most is the illusion of control.

We replay past events, wishing they had gone differently.

We hold onto anger, hoping it will change the past.

We refuse to move on, believing it gives us power.

But the only thing we control is what we do next.

Let go of what you cannot change.

Focus on what you can create.

That is how you reclaim your life.

The Life I Almost Missed – And the Freedom I Found

If I had died by suicide in 2000, I would have never known:

- The joy of releasing the burdens I once carried.
- The peace of no longer living in my past.
- The freedom of waking up each day with a heart unchained.

I almost let my pain define me forever.

But instead, I let it go.

And that? That changed everything.

Your Letting Go Action Plan

📝 **What is one thing I am ready to release?**

_____

📝 **What belief about myself no longer serves me?**

_____

📝 **Who do I need to forgive (including myself)?**

_____

📝 **How will my life improve once I let this go?**

_____

Letting go is a process. **Be patient. Be kind to yourself.**

But most importantly—**choose to start.**

Set Yourself Free

You have carried this weight for long enough.

You have held onto this pain for too many years.

But now, it's time to let go.

Because the future you want? It is waiting for you.

Because the peace you deserve? It is yours to claim.

Because the life you are meant to live? It begins the moment you decide to release the past.

Let it go.

And set yourself free.

Chapter 13:

The Power of Purpose – Turning Pain into Passion

Why Purpose Changes Everything

For years, I believed my pain was meaningless.

I thought my bipolar disorder was just something I had to suffer through.

I thought my suicidal thoughts were proof that I was broken.

I thought my past trauma was just a weight I would carry forever.

But then I discovered something that changed my life: Purpose.

Purpose is the difference between existing and truly living.

It's what gives us a reason to wake up every morning, even when life feels hard.

It's what transforms our pain into something meaningful.

I have seen it in my own life.

- The pain that almost killed me is now the reason I fight for others.
- The darkness I thought would never end is now the light I share with the world.
- The suffering I endured is now the foundation of my purpose.

Your pain is not meaningless. Your story is not over. And your purpose is waiting for you.

My Story – From Suffering to Purpose

I almost didn't get to live this life.

On September 25, 2000, I believed I had no purpose, no future, no way forward. I jumped from the Golden Gate Bridge because I thought my pain would never end. But the second my hands left the rail, I knew I had made the biggest mistake of my life.

I survived.

And I didn't just survive—I found a reason to live.

At first, I didn't know what that reason was. I struggled. I stumbled. I faced setbacks.

But then, something happened: I started sharing my story.

At first, it was terrifying. What if people judged me? What if they didn't understand?

But then something even more powerful happened: People connected.

- They told me, *"Your story helped me keep going."*
- They said, *"Because you survived, I believe I can survive too."*
- They reminded me that my pain wasn't just pain—it was a message.

I realized my purpose wasn't just to survive.

It was to help others do the same.

And that changed everything.

Why Purpose Matters for Mental Health

Science has proven that having a purpose improves mental health.

People with a sense of purpose:

- ☑ Have lower rates of depression and anxiety

- ☑ Are more resilient in the face of setbacks

- ☑ Experience greater overall happiness and life satisfaction

- ☑ Live longer, healthier lives

Why? Because when you have a purpose:

- You are focused on something bigger than your pain.
- You see challenges as opportunities for growth, not just obstacles.
- You wake up every day knowing your life matters.

Purpose is the anchor that keeps us steady in the storm.

Step 1 – Finding Purpose in Your Pain

I used to believe that my struggles made me weak.

But now, I understand: They made me strong.

- My bipolar disorder taught me resilience.
- My suicidal ideation taught me the importance of mental health advocacy.
- My survival gave me a platform to help others.

What if your pain isn't just suffering?

What if it's a lesson?

A message?

A purpose in disguise?

How to Find Purpose in Your Pain

1. Ask yourself: What have I overcome?
2. Who could benefit from my story or experiences?
3. What lessons have my struggles taught me?

When you shift from "Why did this happen to me?" to "How can this help someone else?"—you unlock your purpose.

Step 2 – Identifying What Fulfills You

Purpose doesn't always have to come from pain.

Sometimes, it comes from what lights you up.

Think about the moments when you feel most alive.

- When do you feel truly engaged and passionate?
- What activities make time fly by?
- What do people always come to you for advice on?

For me, speaking and writing became my purpose.

- Every time I stand in front of an audience and share my journey, I feel alive.
- Every time I receive a message from someone saying my words helped them, I feel fulfilled.
- Every time I use my past to help someone else's future, I know I'm exactly where I need to be.

Your purpose is already inside you. You just have to uncover it.

Step 3 – Taking Small Steps Toward Purpose

Finding purpose isn't about making one big change.

It's about small, consistent steps that move you closer to what makes you feel alive.

How to Take Small Steps Toward Purpose:

- ✓ Volunteer for a cause that resonates with you.
- ✓ Start writing, creating, or sharing your message.
- ✓ Mentor someone who is going through what you went through.
- ✓ Turn a hobby into something meaningful.

Purpose doesn't have to be a career.

It doesn't have to be grand.

It just has to mean something to you.

The Life I Almost Missed – And the Purpose I Found

If I had died in 2000, I would have missed:

- My wedding day—standing at the altar, looking into Margaret's eyes, knowing I had found my soulmate.
- The moment I stepped onto a stage for the first time, sharing my story with people who needed to hear it.
- Every conversation with someone who said, "Your story saved my life."
- The realization that my pain didn't end me—it gave me purpose.

I almost missed it all.

But because I stayed, because I fought, because I found my reason to live—I am here, thriving.

And so can you.

Step 4 – Overcoming Fear and Doubt

When I first started speaking, I was terrified.

I thought:

- *"What if no one cares about my story?"*
- *"What if I fail?"*
- *"What if I'm not good enough?"*

But then I realized something:

Fear and doubt are signs that you are stepping into something important.

Every person who has ever done something meaningful has faced fear.

The difference?

They didn't let fear stop them.

Neither should you.

Your Purpose Action Plan

💡 Write down three things that make you feel alive.

💡 Identify one way you can help others using your experience.

💡 Take one small step today toward a purpose-driven life.

Your purpose doesn't have to be big. It just has to matter to you.

Your Life Has Meaning

There was a time I thought my life had no meaning.

Now, I wake up every day with purpose.

Now, I know my struggles weren't wasted.

Now, I understand that I was meant to be here.

And so are you.

- Your pain is not meaningless.
- Your life is not a mistake.
- Your purpose is waiting for you.

Keep going.

Because the future you don't see yet? It is worth staying for.

Chapter 14

The Power of Self-Compassion – Learning to Love Yourself Again

Why Self-Compassion Is the Foundation of Healing

For most of my life, I was my own worst enemy.

- I criticized myself for every mistake.
- I blamed myself for my struggles.
- I thought that because I had bipolar disorder, I was somehow less than.

I held myself to an impossible standard. I showed kindness to others but none to myself. But here's the truth: Healing doesn't happen without self-compassion. You can do all the right things—go to therapy, take your medication, exercise, eat well—but if you are constantly beating yourself up, nothing will ever feel like enough.

Self-compassion is the missing piece.

It's what allows you to:

- ✓ Forgive yourself for your past.
- ✓ Be patient with your progress.
- ✓ See yourself as worthy, just as you are.

And until you start treating yourself with the same kindness you'd give a friend, true healing will always feel just out of reach.

My Story – Learning to Forgive Myself

I have done things I regret.

I have made decisions in manic episodes that hurt people I love.

I have said things in moments of depression that I wish I could take back.

I have been in places so dark that I truly believed the world would be better off without me.

For years, I carried guilt and shame.

- Guilt for the pain I put my family through.
- Guilt for the people who cared about me, who tried to help, but I pushed away.
- Guilt for surviving when so many others didn't.

I thought if I just punished myself enough, I could make up for my mistakes.

But shame does not lead to healing. It leads to suffering.

It wasn't until I started practicing self-compassion—until I truly forgave myself—that I began to heal.

And if I can learn to forgive myself, so can you.

What Is Self-Compassion?

Self-compassion is NOT:

✖ Ignoring your mistakes

✖ Making excuses

✗ Letting yourself off the hook for harmful behavior

Self-compassion IS:

☑ Recognizing that you are human

☑ Understanding that healing takes time

☑ Treating yourself with the same love and patience you give to others

Imagine if you talked to a friend the way you talk to yourself.

Would you ever say:

- *"You're worthless."*
- *"You're never going to get better."*
- *"You don't deserve love."*

No.

So why do you say it to yourself?

Your brain listens to the words you tell it. Choose them wisely.

The Science Behind Self-Compassion

Psychologists have studied self-compassion and found that it is linked to:

☁ Lower levels of anxiety and depression

♥ Greater emotional resilience

🔄 Improved ability to bounce back from setbacks

✺ Increased motivation and self-worth

Why? Because when you are kind to yourself, you reduce stress and emotional suffering.

When you stop fighting yourself, you can start focusing on true healing.

Self-compassion doesn't make you weak. It makes you STRONG.

Step 1 – Changing Your Inner Dialogue

For years, my inner voice was my worst critic.

I had to retrain my brain to be my biggest supporter instead.

How to Change Your Self-Talk:

🔔 **Catch the Criticism** – When you have a negative thought about yourself, pause.

🔄 **Flip the Script** – Replace it with a compassionate thought.

💬 **Use Gentle Language** – Instead of "I'm such a failure," say "I'm doing the best I can."

Example:

✖ "I'll never get better." → ✅ "Healing is a journey, and I am taking steps every day."

✖ "I'm too broken." → ✅ "I am a work in progress, and that's okay."

✖ "I don't deserve love." → ✅ "I am worthy of love just as I am."

You may not believe these words at first. But the more you say them, the more your brain will accept them as truth.

Step 2 – Practicing Radical Self-Forgiveness

I know what it's like to hate yourself for things you can't change.

I know what it's like to lie awake at night, replaying every mistake, every regret, every wrong turn.

But here's what I've learned: You cannot move forward if you are chained to the past.

Forgiveness is not about erasing the past.

It's about giving yourself permission to heal.

How to Practice Self-Forgiveness:

1. Acknowledge what happened. You can't heal what you refuse to face.
2. Take responsibility, but don't punish yourself. Guilt helps us learn. Shame keeps us stuck.
3. Remind yourself that you are not your past. Every day is a chance to be better.

If you wouldn't hold someone else to an impossible standard, why do you hold yourself to one?

Step 3 – The Power of Self-Care as Self-Compassion

Self-care isn't just about bubble baths and relaxation.

It's about showing yourself that you are worth the effort.

Ways to Practice Self-Care with Compassion:

♥ **Move your body** – Not to "fix" yourself, but to honor your health.

♥ **Eat nourishing foods** – Not as punishment, but as self-respect.

♥ **Set boundaries** – Protect your peace by saying no when you need to.

♥ **Rest without guilt** – You do not have to "earn" rest. You deserve it.

Every time you take care of yourself; you send a message to your brain:

"I matter. I am worth it."

The Life I Almost Missed – And the Love I Found for Myself

If I had died by suicide in 2000, I would have missed:

- Falling in love with Margaret, my wife, my heart, my best friend.
- The joy of learning that I am not my diagnosis.
- Every moment of laughter, every hug, every victory over my own mind.
- The realization that I am worthy—not because of what I do, but because of who I am.

I almost let self-hatred take my future away.

But I chose self-compassion instead.

And that choice saved my life.

Your Self-Compassion Action Plan

♥ Write down three kind things about yourself.

♥ When negative self-talk appears, replace it with a positive truth.

♥ Practice one act of self-care today—without guilt.

♥ Forgive yourself for one thing you've been holding onto.

You do not have to be perfect. You just have to be kind to yourself.

You Deserve Your Own Love

If you take nothing else from this chapter, take this:

You deserve your own love.

Not when you "fix" yourself.

Not when you reach some imaginary standard.

Not when you finally feel "good enough."

Right now. Just as you are.

Because the truth is, you have always been enough.

And the moment you start believing that? Everything changes.

Chapter 15:

Mastering Brain Health, Physical Health, and Overall Well-Being – The Work of a Lifetime

The Myth of Instant Wellness

We live in a world where everything is designed for instant gratification.

- Want food? Order it.
- Need a ride? Request it.
- Want to feel better? Take a pill, watch a motivational video, do a quick hack.

But here's the truth that no one likes to hear:

There is no Uber for mental and physical wellness.

You cannot download an app and wake up healed.

You cannot watch a single TED Talk and suddenly have all the answers.

You cannot snap your fingers and erase the years of struggle.

Wellness requires work.

Healing requires effort.

Strength—mental and physical—is earned over time.

And while that may sound intimidating, here's the good news:

You can do the work.

You can master your health.

You can build a life that feels good to wake up to.

This chapter is about doing the work—step by step, day by day—so that your brain, body, and soul become stronger than ever before. Because nothing worth having ever came easy. And nothing great was ever built without effort.

My Story – The Work I Had to Do to Stay Alive

I won't sugarcoat it—staying alive was hard.

After my suicide attempt, I didn't magically wake up with a new mindset. I didn't suddenly feel grateful for life. I didn't instantly know how to take care of myself.

What happened was this: I decided to fight for my life.

And that decision required:

- Time. Nothing changed overnight. I had to be patient.
- Effort. I had to put in the work every single day.
- Energy. Some days, I had to force myself to move, to get out of bed, to keep going.
- Hard Work. No shortcuts, no hacks—just consistent action toward getting better.

Some days, the work was brutal.

But I learned that the hardest things in life are often the most worth it.

Mastering Brain Health – It's Not Just Mental, It's Physical

For too long, mental health has been treated separately from physical health. But science tells us:

🛆 **Brain health IS physical health.**

Your brain is an organ, just like your heart. If you want a healthy mind, you need to take care of your brain the same way you take care of your body.

How to Strengthen Your Brain:

☁ **Eat Brain-Boosting Foods** – Omega-3s, antioxidants, whole foods (not processed junk).

☁ **Move Daily** – Exercise increases blood flow to the brain, boosting cognitive function.

☁ **Sleep Well** – Sleep is the brain's reset button. No sleep = poor emotional regulation.

☁ **Challenge Your Mind** – Read, learn, do puzzles—keep your brain sharp.

Brain health isn't just about thoughts and emotions. It's about how you fuel, move, and rest your body. If you want to master your mental wellness, start with mastering your brain health.

Mastering Physical Health – Strength from the Inside Out

Your body is the foundation of everything. If you feel physically weak, exhausted, and drained, your mind will struggle too. The best thing I ever did for my mental health was getting serious about my physical health.

- I started moving my body every day.
- I changed my diet to fuel, not punish, my body.
- I committed to rest and recovery, not burnout.

Your Body is Your Powerhouse – Treat it Like One

- ✓ Fuel it wisely – Nutrient-dense foods, hydration, NO overloading on sugar and processed junk.
- ✓ Strengthen it – Lift, move, stretch—your body was built to be active.
- ✓ Respect its limits – Rest is just as important as movement.
- ✓ Listen to it – Pain, fatigue, brain fog? Your body is telling you something—don't ignore it.

Physical health is not about perfection. It's about building a body that can support the life you want to live.

The Work Never Stops – And That's a Good Thing

Some people say, *"How long does it take to be mentally and physically strong?"*

The answer? Forever.

You don't hit a magic point where you never struggle again.

You don't reach some finish line where wellness is complete.

Because wellness isn't a destination. It's a lifelong process.

But don't let that discourage you. Let it empower you.

Because every day, you get the chance to improve.

Every day, you can make small choices that lead to big transformations.

Every day, you can put in the work to be stronger than you were yesterday.

And there is something incredibly powerful and freeing about knowing that YOU are in control.

Why There Are No Shortcuts to True Wellness

People are always searching for the quick fix.

They want the instant mental health cure.

They want the overnight fitness transformation.

They want the easy way out.

But here's the truth: There is no shortcut to a strong mind or a strong body.

You cannot:

- ✖ Think positive thoughts and expect your life to change overnight.
- ✖ Take a supplement and suddenly be mentally resilient.
- ✖ Skip the work and expect lasting results.

The only path to true wellness is time, effort, energy, and hard work.

If it were easy, everyone would be thriving.

If it were instant, everyone would be mentally unbreakable.

But the people who are truly strong—mentally, physically, and emotionally—are the ones who put in the work, day after day, no matter how hard it gets.

Step 1 – The Daily Wellness Blueprint

The best way to build long-term mental and physical strength? Consistency.

Daily Non-Negotiables for Mastering Wellness:

- ✓ 30 Minutes of Movement – Walk, lift, stretch—just move.
- ✓ Brain-Boosting Nutrition – Eat for fuel, not just for convenience.
- ✓ Daily Mindset Work – Read, reflect, or practice gratitude.
- ✓ Intentional Rest – Sleep and recovery are just as important as action.

When you do these things consistently, you become unstoppable.

The Life I Almost Missed – And the Strength I Built

If I had died in 2000, I would have missed:

- The chance to become strong, inside and out.
- The joy of feeling in control of my own health.
- The proof that with work, anything is possible.
- The ability to help others build their own strength.

I almost gave up before I realized my greatest potential.

But now, I know I was meant to be here. I was meant to be strong.

And so are you.

Your Action Plan – Building Strength in Every Area

💪 What's one small action you can take today for your brain health?

💪 What's one way you can improve your physical health this week?

💪 What's one thing you can commit to doing consistently—no matter what?

The work is hard. But it is worth it.

The Strength is in the Work

There is no instant path to true wellness.

There is no shortcut to strength.

There is no easy way to master your mind and body.

But you know what?

That's what makes it worth it.

Because when you put in the work—when you fight for your life, your health, your future—

You become unbreakable.

And that? That is worth everything.

Chapter 16:

Resilience – The Art of Bouncing Back Stronger

Why Resilience Is the Key to Everything

Life is not easy.

It will knock you down.

It will test you.

It will put obstacles in your path that seem impossible to overcome.

But the people who thrive—the ones who find real, lasting wellness—are not the ones who never face hardship.

They are the ones who refuse to stay down.

That's what resilience is.

- It's getting back up when life knocks you down.
- It's refusing to let your past dictate your future.
- It's looking at your struggles and saying, "You will not break me."

And the most powerful thing about resilience?

It is a skill you can build.

You don't have to be born with it.

You don't have to be naturally "tough."

You just have to choose to keep going.

Because the truth is, resilience is not about never falling—it's about getting back up every single time.

My Story – The Hardest Thing I Ever Had to Do

I know what it feels like to hit rock bottom.

- To feel like you have nothing left to give.
- To believe that the pain will never end.
- To think that giving up is the only way out.

I believed that on September 25, 2000, when I jumped from the Golden Gate Bridge.

But what I didn't know in that moment was this:

I was stronger than I thought.

- Strong enough to fight for my life as I fell.
- Strong enough to survive the impact.
- Strong enough to endure the pain, the surgeries, the mental and physical recovery.

And strong enough to keep going.

There were days I wanted to quit.

Days I didn't think I would ever get better.

Days where my mind told me, "This is too hard. You should just give up."

But resilience isn't about never having those thoughts.

It's about pushing forward anyway.

And the day I truly understood that—the day I decided to be resilient, no matter what— was the day my life changed forever.

The Science of Resilience – How It Changes Your Brain

Resilience is not just a mindset.

It physically changes your brain.

When you build resilience:

🧠 Your prefrontal cortex (the part of your brain that controls decision-making) becomes stronger.

♡ Your amygdala (the fear center) becomes less reactive, helping you manage stress better.

💡 Your brain builds new neural pathways, making it easier to adapt to challenges.

In other words, the more you practice resilience, the easier it becomes.

Every time you push through a tough moment, you are literally rewiring your brain to be stronger.

And that is the definition of true power.

Step 1 – Learning to Reframe Setbacks

Setbacks are not the enemy. They are part of the process.

Every strong person has faced failure.

Every success story is built on a foundation of setbacks.

How to Reframe Setbacks as Lessons

🚀 Instead of *"I failed,"* say *"I learned something valuable."*

🚀 Instead of *"This is the end,"* say *"This is just a chapter in my story."*

🚀 Instead of *"I can't do this,"* say *"I haven't figured it out yet."*

When you change the way you see setbacks, you take away their power over you. Don't even call them failures, call them step ups to something greater. As long as you keep going a "FAILURE" is irrelevant!

Step 2 – Building Mental Toughness

Resilience is not about ignoring emotions or pretending everything is fine.

It is about learning to navigate difficulty without letting it break you.

How to Build Mental Toughness

- ✓ Practice gratitude, even in the hard times.
- ✓ Develop a "bounce-back" routine (something you do when things go wrong).
- ✓ Train yourself to find solutions instead of dwelling on problems.
- ✓ Remind yourself that you have survived 100% of your worst days.

Tough times don't last. But tough people do.

Step 3 – The Role of Self-Discipline in Resilience

People think resilience is about motivation.

It's not.

Motivation is fleeting. Discipline is what keeps you going.

There will be days when you don't feel like showing up.

Days when you want to quit.

Days when your emotions try to take over.

That's when discipline kicks in.

How to Stay Disciplined When Life Gets Hard

1. Have a "WHY" bigger than your excuses.
2. Create non-negotiable daily habits that keep you moving forward.
3. Surround yourself with people who hold you accountable.
4. Remind yourself that every small action builds resilience.

The strongest people in the world are not the ones who never struggle.

They are the ones who keep showing up, no matter what.

Step 4 – The Power of Hope in Resilience

Hope is not just a feeling.

It is a strategy.

When I was struggling, I used to think hope was just wishful thinking. But I was wrong.

Hope is what keeps you going when things seem impossible.

Hope is what allows you to see beyond your current pain.

Hope is what reminds you that things will get better—even if you don't see how yet.

How to Hold onto Hope During Hard Times

💡 Look for proof that things can improve. (If others have survived tough times, so can you.)

💡 Visualize a future where you are thriving.

💡 Remind yourself of past struggles you overcame.

💡 Take one small action every day that moves you forward.

Hope is not passive. It is an active choice.

And choosing hope, repeatedly, is one of the strongest things you can do.

The Life I Almost Missed – And the Strength I Built

If I had died in 2000, I would have missed:

- The chance to prove to myself that I could survive anything.
- The joy of seeing how much stronger I became over time.
- The opportunity to help others find their own resilience.
- The realization that my struggles didn't break me—they built me.

I almost let one moment of despair steal an entire lifetime of strength.

But I didn't.

I chose to fight.

I chose to keep going.

I chose resilience.

And so can you.

Your Resilience Action Plan

💪 Write down three times in your life when you showed resilience.

💪 Reframe one current challenge as an opportunity for growth.

💪 Commit to one action every day that builds your mental strength.

💪 Choose hope, even when it's hard.

You are stronger than you think.

You are more capable than you know.

And no matter what happens, you will get back up.

You Are Unbreakable

Resilience is not about never falling.

It is about always rising.

- No matter how many times life knocks you down… you can get back up.
- No matter how impossible things seem… you can keep going.
- No matter how much pain you've faced… you can build a future that is worth fighting for.

Because you are unbreakable.

And that?

That changes everything.

Chapter 17:

Unbreakable – The Strength Within You

What It Means to Be Unbreakable

Life will test you.

It will throw storms your way.

It will push you to the edge and make you question everything.

But no matter what happens, there is one undeniable truth:

You are stronger than you think.

Being unbreakable doesn't mean life doesn't hurt.

It doesn't mean you never struggle.

It doesn't mean you never feel pain.

Being unbreakable means:

💪 You keep going, even when it's hard.

💪 You refuse to let adversity define you.

💪 You take your pain and turn it into strength.

I know this because I've lived it.

And I know this because I have met countless others who have done the same. This chapter is about becoming unbreakable—not by avoiding hardship, but by learning to rise from it, stronger than ever before.

My Story – How I Turned Adversity into Strength

There was a time I believed I was broken.

I lived with bipolar disorder and thought it made me weak.

I struggled with suicidal thoughts and believed I had no future.

I jumped from the Golden Gate Bridge, convinced my life had no meaning.

But I was wrong.

Because the very things that almost destroyed me? They became the foundation of my strength.

- Bipolar disorder didn't break me. It made me resilient.
- My darkest days didn't end me. They showed me how strong I really am.
- My survival wasn't just luck. It was proof that I was meant to be here.

I took the very thing that almost killed me and turned it into my life's mission.

I became a suicide prevention advocate.

I became a speaker, an author, a mental health warrior.

I became a man who wakes up every day knowing his purpose.

My pain did not break me. It did not destroy me…It built me.

And no matter what you've been through, you can do the same.

Lessons from People Who Have Overcome the Impossible

I am not the only one who has turned pain into power.

I have met warriors—people who have faced unimaginable suffering and still chose to fight.

A Soldier Who Lost His Legs, But Not His Spirit

I once met a soldier who had lost both legs in combat.

He could have given up.

He could have let his loss define him.

Instead, he became an athlete. **A man filled with motivation. A leader.**

He told me:

"Pain is inevitable. Suffering is optional, it's a choice. I chose to rise."

A Woman Who Survived Abuse and Became a Voice for Others

I met a woman who had survived horrific abuse.

She could have let the past consume her.

Instead, she became an advocate, a voice for others who felt voiceless.

She said:

"What happened to me was not my fault. But what I do next? That's my power."

A Teen Who Survived a Suicide Attempt and Found His Purpose

I spoke to a young man who had survived a suicide attempt. He believed his life was over.

But after surviving, he realized:

"I didn't die because I was meant to live. And now, I help others do the same. Your story Kevin saved my life!"

What These Stories Teach Us:

- Adversity is not the end of the story.
- Pain can either destroy you or build you—your choice.
- Strength is found in those who refuse to give up.

If they can rise, so can you.

How to Live a Purpose-Driven Life

Purpose is what makes you unbreakable.

When you have a reason to wake up every morning, nothing can stop you.

But many people ask me:

"How do I find my purpose?"

The answer?

You don't find it. You build it.

Steps to Create a Purpose-Driven Life:

Look at Your Pain – What have you overcome? Your biggest struggles often point to your purpose.

Ask Yourself: Who Can I Help? – Your purpose is not just about you. It's about using your experiences to make a difference.

Take Action – Even small steps—volunteering, mentoring, speaking out—can lead to a bigger mission.

Stay Committed – Purpose isn't always easy, but it's what keeps you going when life gets tough.

I turned my pain into purpose.

And you can do the same.

Why You Are Stronger Than You Think

Right now, you might not feel strong.

You might feel tired.

You might feel overwhelmed.

You might feel like life keeps knocking you down.

But let me remind you of something:

You have survived 100% of your worst days.

You are still here.

You are still fighting.

And that? That is proof of your strength.

Signs You Are Stronger Than You Think:

- ✓ You've faced hard times—and you're still standing.
- ✓ You've battled your mind—and you keep showing up.
- ✓ You've fallen—but you refuse to stay down.

You don't need to be fearless.

You don't need to have all the answers.

You just need to keep going.

Step 1 – Building an Unbreakable Mindset

Your mind is your greatest weapon.

The way you talk to yourself, the thoughts you feed, the beliefs you hold—they shape your reality.

How to Strengthen Your Mindset:

💡 **Challenge Negative Thoughts** – Replace "I can't" with "I will figure this out."

💡 **Embrace Discomfort** – Growth happens outside your comfort zone.

💡 **Focus on Progress, Not Perfection** – Strength is built over time.

💡 **Surround Yourself with Fighters** – Your environment shapes your mindset.

The stronger your mindset, the more unbreakable you become.

Step 2 – How to Keep Going When Life Gets Hard

Some days, motivation disappears.

Some days, you will feel like quitting.

Here's how to keep pushing forward:

- ✓ Remember Your "Why" – Remind yourself why you started.
- ✓ Break It Down – Take life one step at a time.
- ✓ Ask for Help – Strength is knowing when to lean on others.
- ✓ Never Quit on a Bad Day – Hard moments don't define the future.

Tough times are temporary. Your strength is permanent.

The Life I Almost Missed – And the Strength I Found

If I had died in 2000, I would have missed:

- The chance to prove I was stronger than my pain.
- The joy of living a purpose-driven life.
- The realization that struggles don't break us—they build us.

I almost **let one moment of weakness** define my entire life.

But instead, I chose strength.

I chose resilience.

I chose to be unbreakable.

And if I can do it, so can you.

Your Unbreakable Action Plan

🔥 Write down three ways you have shown strength in your life.

🔥 Reframe one challenge as an opportunity for growth.

🔥 Commit to one action that moves you closer to a purpose-driven life.

🔥 Decide, right now, that you will never give up on yourself.

You Were Made for More

You are not weak.

You are not broken.

You are not defeated.

You are strong.

You are worthy.

You are unbreakable.

And the future is waiting for you?

It is worth every battle, every challenge, and every moment of struggle.

Keep going. Keep fighting. Keep rising.

Because your story is far from over.

Chapter 18:

The Greatest Gift – Living to Give Back

Life Is About More Than Survival

For so long, my only goal was survival.

After my suicide attempt, I was just trying to make it through each day.

I wasn't thinking about my purpose. I wasn't thinking about giving back.

I was just trying to stay alive.

And that's okay.

If you're in survival mode right now, stay. Keep fighting. Keep pushing forward.

Because survival is the first step. But it is not the end of the story.

At some point, survival is no longer enough.

Because we are not just meant to survive.

We are meant to thrive.

We are meant to give.

We are meant to leave this world better than we found it.

That is the greatest gift of all:

Once we heal, we must turn around and help others heal, too.

My Story – The Moment I Knew I Had to Give Back

I will never forget the first time I told my story in public.

I stood on a stage, nervous, heart pounding, questioning why I was even there.

Then, after I finished speaking, a young man approached me.

He looked me in the eyes and said, "Because you survived, I believe I can, too."

I realized something in that moment:

My survival wasn't just for me.

My pain, my struggles, my near-death experience—they weren't just random suffering.

They were meant to be shared.

They were meant to help someone else.

And from that day forward, I knew my life was not just mine.

It belonged to every person who needed to hear my story.

Every person who was struggling alone.

Every person who needed proof that they could survive, too.

The Purpose of Life – Becoming a Beacon for Others

We all go through pain.

We all have dark chapters.

We all face battles that seem impossible to win.

But once we find the light, it is our job to share it.

The Cycle of Healing and Giving Back

1. First, you survive. You fight through the pain. You make it.

2. Then, you heal. You do the work. You grow. You transform.

3. Finally, you give back. You take what you've learned and help someone else.

This is how the world changes—not by waiting for someone else to fix it, but by each of us stepping up and being the person, we once needed.

The Unexpected Beauty of a Life Lived for Others

When I was deep in my suffering, I never imagined a life like this.

- I never imagined waking up excited to help others.
- I never imagined traveling the world, sharing my story.
- I never imagined that the thing that almost ended me would become my greatest gift.

Why Giving Back Changes Everything

- ✓ It turns your pain into power.
- ✓ It reminds you that your struggles were not wasted.
- ✓ It gives your life meaning beyond just yourself.
- ✓ It keeps you going, even on hard days.

The greatest joy you will ever experience is knowing you made someone else's life better.

That is what makes life worth living.

The People Who Prove That Giving Back is the Ultimate Purpose

I have met warriors—people who faced unthinkable suffering and turned it into something beautiful.

The Veteran Who Dedicated His Life to Helping Others

I met a soldier who struggled with PTSD after war.

For years, he thought his pain was meaningless.

Then, he started speaking out.

He built a program for struggling veterans.

He **turned his trauma into a mission.**

He told me:

"If I made it through hell, it's my duty to help others do the same."

The Woman Who Escaped an Abusive Home and Now Helps Survivors

She could have stayed silent.

She could have run from the past.

Instead, she became a voice for others.

She started a foundation that has helped thousands.

She told me:

"I am free now. But my real purpose is making sure others find their freedom, too."

The Teen Who Survived a Suicide Attempt and Became a Mental Health Advocate

He thought his life was over.

Now, he stands on stages telling his story, saving lives.

He told me:

"I tried to die. But now, I wake up every day knowing I am here to help someone else live."

Their stories are proof of one thing:

The best way to find yourself is to serve others.

How to Live a Life of Purpose and Service

You don't have to be famous.

You don't have to have a platform.

You don't have to have all the answers.

You just have to care.

Ways to Give Back Today

- ✓ **Share your story.** Someone out there needs to hear it.
- ✓ **Volunteer.** A small act of kindness can change a life.
- ✓ **Mentor someone.** Be the guide you wish you had.
- ✓ **Listen.** Sometimes, people just need to be heard.
- ✓ **Live your truth.** Your example alone can inspire others.

You don't have to change the whole world.

But you can change someone's world.

And that? That is everything.

The Life I Almost Missed – And the Purpose I Found

If I had died in 2000, I would have missed:

- The joy of waking up every day knowing my life matters.
- The thousands of people I have helped find hope.
- The purpose I never imagined I would find.
- The love I share with Margaret, my wife, my heart, my reason.

I almost threw it all away.

But now I know:

I was saved so I could help others.

And if you are reading this, so were you.

The Unwritten Future – The Next Chapter is Yours

This book has been about building a life worth living.

Now, the question is:

What will you do with your life?

You have survived.

You have fought through pain.

You have learned how to be strong.

Now, it's time to step into your purpose.

Because the world needs you.

Someone out there needs you.

Your life is meant for more than just you.

So go.

Give.

Make a difference.

And never forget: You were born for this.

Your Action Plan – Turning Your Life into a Legacy

📝 What have you learned from your struggles?

📝 How can you use that lesson to help others?

📝 What is one thing you can do this week to give back?

📝 Commit, right now, to being the person you once needed.

Because the greatest legacy you can leave is a life lived for others.

The Message – Your Life Matters More Than You Know

If you take nothing else from this book, take this:

Your life is a gift.

Your struggles are part of your story.

And your purpose is waiting for you.

So, live boldly.

Love deeply.

Give freely.

Because the greatest meaning of life is found in lifting others up.

And if you are here, you have something to give.

You are here for a reason.

Now go live that reason.

"The meaning of life is not just to heal ourselves, but to use our healing to lift others up. Because once we find our way out of the darkness, it is our responsibility to turn around and light the way for someone else." – Kevin Hines

This is The Art of Wellness

This book is complete, but your journey is just beginning.

Now go. Live. Thrive. Give.

Because you were meant for more.

🚀 Onward. 🚀

The Art of Wellness: Interactive Workbook

Introduction: Your Journey to Wellness Starts Here

This workbook is designed to help you track your mental, emotional, and physical wellness as you apply the lessons from The Art of Wellness. Use it as your personal journal, a space for reflection, and a tool for growth.

Take your time. Healing is not a race. This is YOUR journey.

Chapter 1:
Understanding Mental Fitness

Reflection Questions:

1. How do you currently define "mental fitness" in your life?
2. What are three challenges that prevent you from feeling mentally strong?
3. Describe a moment when you felt mentally resilient.

Action Steps:

- Write down one small action you can take every day to improve your mental fitness:

_____

_____

_____

_____

Chapter 2:
Breaking Free from Labels

Reflection & Reframing:

1. A label I have placed on myself is
   _____.

2. A label other has placed on me is
   _____.

3. I will redefine myself as because
   _____.

Journaling Prompt:

- How has labeling affected the way you see yourself? How can you shift from a victim mindset to an empowerment mindset?

_____

_____

_____

_____

Chapter 3:
Nutrition and the Brain

Wellness Tracker:

- Did you eat foods that fuel your brain today? Yes / No
- What did you eat that made you feel energized?
  _____

- What foods made you feel sluggish?
  _____

Goal Setting:

- This week, I will focus on eating more:

  _____

- This week, I will reduce my intake of:

  _____

  _____

Chapter 4:
Exercise for the Mind and Body

Physical and Mental Health Log:

- Did you move your body today? Yes / No
- What activity did you do?
  _____

- How did you feel after?
  _____

Weekly Challenge:

- Set a movement goal for the next seven days:

_____

_____

Chapter 5:
Sleep as Medicine

Sleep Tracker:

Day	Hours of Sleep	Sleep Quality (1-10)	Notes
Monday			
Tuesday			
Wednesday			
Thursday			
Friday			
Saturday			
Sunday			

Reflection:

- What is one habit I can change to improve my sleep?

_____

_____

Chapter 6:
Mindfulness and Meditation

Daily Mindfulness Log:

- Today, I practiced mindfulness by:
  _____

- A moment I truly felt present was:
  _____

- One thing I noticed about my thoughts today was:
  _____

  _____

Chapter 7:
Emotional Intelligence

Emotional Check-In:

- Today, I felt: (circle all that apply)
  - Happy - Sad - Anxious - Excited - Stressed - Confident - Angry - Peaceful - Other: _____

- What triggered this emotion?
  _____

- How did I respond to this emotion?
  _____

Self-Regulation Strategy:

- One healthy way I can manage difficult emotions is _____.
  _____

Chapter 8:
Social Connection

Building My Support System:

- Who are the three people I can turn to for support?

1. _____
2. _____
3. _____

- Who in my life might need support from me right now?

_____

Action Step:

- This week, I will connect with someone by

_____.

_____

Chapter 9-18 Fill-in-the-Blank Sections

Chapter 9:
The Power of Purpose

- A struggle I have overcome is:
  _____
- Someone who might benefit from my story is:
  _____
- A cause I feel passionate about is:
  _____

Chapter 10:
Mastering Brain and Physical Health

- A wellness goal I am committed to:
  _____
- One daily action to support this goal:
  _____

Chapter 11:
Resilience

- A setback I faced recently and how I overcame it:
  _____

- One lesson I learned from this experience:
  _____

Chapter 12:
The Art of Letting Go

- Something I've been holding onto that I need to release:
  _____

- How will letting go improve my life?
  _____

Chapter 13:

Becoming Unbreakable

- What personal struggle made me stronger?

  _____

Chapter 14:

The Power of Self-Compassion

- How can I show myself more kindness daily?

  _____

Chapter 15:

Mastering Wellness Through Effort

- One area of my wellness where I need to put in more effort:

  _____

Chapter 16:

Resilience – Bouncing Back Stronger

- How have I built resilience in my life?

  _____

Chapter 17:

Living with Purpose

- A way I can give back to others:

  _____

Chapter 18:

The Greatest Gift – Giving Back

- What legacy do I want to leave behind?

  _____

  _____

Daily Readers Journal: 30-Day Wellness Tracker

Instructions:

Use this space to reflect daily on your progress, successes, brain pain, and struggles. Be honest with yourself. Track your thoughts, emotions, and any insights as you apply the lessons from The Art of Wellness to your life. This is a safe space for self-growth and healing.

_____

Day 1

Today, I felt: _____

What was a success today?

_____

What was a challenge or struggle?

_____

What did I learn about my mental and physical wellness?

_____

_____

Day 2

Today, I felt: _____

What was a success today?

_____

What was a challenge or struggle?

_____

What did I learn about my mental and physical wellness?

_____

_____

Day 3

Today, I felt: _____

What was a success today?

_____

What was a challenge or struggle?

_____

What did I learn about my mental and physical wellness?

_____

_____

Day 4

Today, I felt: _____

What was a success today?

_____

What was a challenge or struggle?

_____

What did I learn about my mental and physical wellness?

_____

_____

Day 5

Today, I felt: _____

What was a success today?

_____

What was a challenge or struggle?

_____

What did I learn about my mental and physical wellness?

_____

_____

Day 6

Today, I felt: _____

What was a success today?

_____

What was a challenge or struggle?

_____

What did I learn about my mental and physical wellness?

_____

_____

Day 7

Today, I felt: _____

What was a success today?

_____

What was a challenge or struggle?

_____

What did I learn about my mental and physical wellness?

_____

_____

Day 8

Today, I felt: _____

What was a success today?

_____

What was a challenge or struggle?

_____

What did I learn about my mental and physical wellness?

_____

_____

Day 9

Today, I felt: _____

What was a success today?

_____

What was a challenge or struggle?

_____

What did I learn about my mental and physical wellness?

_____

Day 10

Today, I felt: _____

What was a success today?

_____

What was a challenge or struggle?

_____

What did I learn about my mental and physical wellness?

_____

_____

Day 11

Today, I felt: _____

What was a success today?

_____

What was a challenge or struggle?

_____

What did I learn about my mental and physical wellness?

_____

_____

Day 12

Today, I felt: _____

What was a success today?

_____

What was a challenge or struggle?

_____

What did I learn about my mental and physical wellness?

_____

_____

Day 13

Today, I felt: _____

What was a success today?

_____

What was a challenge or struggle?

_____

What did I learn about my mental and physical wellness?

_____

_____

Day 14

Today, I felt: _____

What was a success today?

_____

What was a challenge or struggle?

_____

What did I learn about my mental and physical wellness?

_____

_____

Day 15

Today, I felt: _____

What was a success today?

_____

What was a challenge or struggle?

_____

What did I learn about my mental and physical wellness?

_____

_____

Day 16

Today, I felt: _____

What was a success today?

_____

What was a challenge or struggle?

_____

What did I learn about my mental and physical wellness?

_____

_____

Day 17

Today, I felt:

_____

What was a success today?

_____

What was a challenge or struggle?

_____

What did I learn about my mental and physical wellness?

_____

_____

Day 18

Today, I felt: _____

What was a success today?

_____

What was a challenge or struggle?

_____

What did I learn about my mental and physical wellness?

_____

_____

Day 19

Today, I felt: _____

What was a success today?

_____

What was a challenge or struggle?

_____

What did I learn about my mental and physical wellness?

_____

_____

Day 20

Today, I felt: _____

What was a success today?

_____

What was a challenge or struggle?

_____

What did I learn about my mental and physical wellness?

_____

_____

Day 21

Today, I felt: _____

What was a success today?

_____

What was a challenge or struggle?

_____

What did I learn about my mental and physical wellness?

_____

_____

Day 22

Today, I felt: _____

What was a success today?

_____

What was a challenge or struggle?

_____

What did I learn about my mental and physical wellness?

_____

_____

Day 23

Today, I felt: _____

What was a success today?

_____

What was a challenge or struggle?

_____

What did I learn about my mental and physical wellness?

_____

Day 24

Today, I felt: _____

What was a success today?

_____

What was a challenge or struggle?

_____

What did I learn about my mental and physical wellness?

_____

_____

Day 25

Today, I felt: _____

What was a success today?

_____

What was a challenge or struggle?

_____

What did I learn about my mental and physical wellness?

_____

_____

Day 26

Today, I felt: _____

What was a success today?

_____

What was a challenge or struggle?

_____

What did I learn about my mental and physical wellness?

_____

_____

Day 27

Today, I felt: _____

What was a success today?

_____

What was a challenge or struggle?

_____

What did I learn about my mental and physical wellness?

_____

_____

Day 28

Today, I felt: _____

What was a success today?

_____

What was a challenge or struggle?

_____

What did I learn about my mental and physical wellness?

_____

_____

Day 29

Today, I felt: _____

What was a success today?

_____

What was a challenge or struggle?

_____

What did I learn about my mental and physical wellness?

_____

_____

_____

Day 30

Today, I felt: _____

What was a success today?

_____

What was a challenge or struggle?

_____

What did I learn about my mental and physical wellness?

_____

_____

Important Reflections

- **Looking back over the past 30 days, what progress have I made?**
  _____

- **What challenges did I overcome?**
  _____

- **How has my perspective on wellness changed?**
  _____

- **What commitment will I make to myself moving forward?**
  _____

🚀 Keep going. Your wellness journey is lifelong and remember…We need you! 🚀

Made in the USA
Coppell, TX
07 March 2026

73327975R00092